A scene from the WPA production of "Jeffrey." Set design by James Youmans.

Photo by Carol Rosegg

JEFFREY

BY PAUL RUDNICK

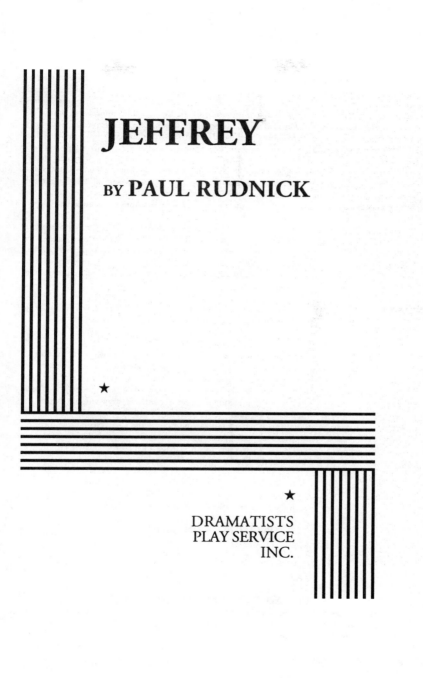

★

★

DRAMATISTS
PLAY SERVICE
INC.

For My Father

INTRODUCTION

JEFFREY is a blend of romantic comedy, wild farce and real emotion; in performance, the play demands speed and dexterity. The stakes must be kept extremely high: the characters, however blithe, are playing for keeps.

JEFFREY is, as he announces, "a naturally cheerful person." He must not be played as neurotic or morose; he is determined to be happy, even if a very justifiable despair pursues him at every turn. Steve is a man who has clearly dealt with the rage and hopelessness which accompany an illness as devastating as AIDS; he has chosen to live a full, happy and romantic life. Even when he accuses Jeffrey of cowardice, his yearning must be evident; he and Jeffrey are deeply in love, and the play should represent their triumph.

The role of Sterling requires verbal agility. Sterling enjoys words, and he adores his friends — he also possesses great moral strength. Darius, his lover, is an innocent; like Steve, he has made a decision to flourish despite his precarious health. Sterling and Darius' love affair is very real; they should be physically comfortable and affectionate with each other, and with Jeffrey and Steve.

JEFFREY was originally performed by an ensemble of eight actors. The actors playing Sterling, Darius and Steve played other roles in the opening bedroom scene, but otherwise did not double. Three actors played all the additional roles, and a single actress played all the women. The pace was lightning-quick, under the superb direction of Christopher Ashley. All of the actors were capable of inspired clowning and at times heartbreaking depth; even in the play's more satiric moments, everything mattered. The higher the emotional stakes of the play the funnier it will be — the play requires urgency and precision, accompanied by high spirits. As designed by James Youmans, the original production used little scenery, a few chairs or a bench, and relied on a series of full-stage projections, often collages, to place the action. We also used a turntable to keep the staging fluid. Other options are possible, but the play should never be burdened by time-consuming scene shifts. We also used a stylized cut-out skyline and a huge, glowing moon for the play's final scene, which lent the moment a wonderful storybook quality.

JEFFREY is a very personal play for me; it is a play about love, death and wisecracks. Audiences often imagine that a comedy about AIDS is impossible; JEFFREY is a tribute to people who battle disease and fear with passion, humor and style.

— Paul Rudnick

JEFFREY received its premeire at the WPA Theatre (Kyle Renick, Artistic Director; Donna Lieberman, Managing Director), in New York City, on December 31, 1992. It was directed by Christopher Ashley; the set design was by James Youmans; the lighting design was by Donald Holder; the costume design was by David C. Woolard; the sound design was by Donna Riley and the production stage manager was John Frederick Sullivan. The cast was as follows:

JEFFREY ....John Michael Higgins
MAN #1 IN BED, GYM RAT, SKIP WINKLY,
CASTING DIRECTOR, WAITER IN HEADDRESS,
MAN #2 WITH DEBRA, MAN IN JOCKSTAP,
   THUG #2, DAVE, ANGELIQUE ....Patrick Kerr
MAN #2 IN BED, GYM RAT, SALESMAN,
THE BOSS, MAN #1 WITH DEBRA, MAN IN CHAPS,
   THUG #1, FATHER JULIAN, SEAN .... Daryl Theirse
MAN #3 IN BED, GYM RAT, DON, TIM,
   DAD, FATHER DAN, CHUCK FARLING ..... Richard Poe
MAN #4 IN BED, DARIUS .... Bryan Batt
MAN #5 IN BED, STERLING .... Edward Hibbert
MAN #6 IN BED, STEVE.. Tom Hewitt
WOMAN IN BED, SHOWGIRL, ANN MARWOOD
BARTLE, DEBRA MOORHOUSE,
MOTHER TERESA, SHARON, MOM
   MRS. MARCANGELO .... Harriet Harris

The WPA production of JEFFREY was moved to the Minetta Lane Theatre (Thomas Viertel, Richard Frankel, Steven Baruch, Jack Viertel, Mitchell Maxwell and Alan Schuster, Producers), in New York City in May, 1993. In this production, the part of MAN #2 IN BED, was played by Scott Whitehurst.

JEFFREY

ACT ONE

The play takes place in a wide variety of locations, all of which should be suggested as simply as possible. The staging should be fast-paced and fluid, always a few steps ahead of the audience.

As the play begins, we see a series of slides projected on the front curtain or scrim, accompanied by lush, moody music such as a Gershwin* score. The slides include various ultraromantic views of the Manhattan skyline, the streets of Greenwich Village, and, finally, the windows of an appealing brownstone. It is late at night.

Jeffrey is in his thirties, attractive and well put-together. He is an innocent; he is outgoing and optimistic, cheerful despite all odds. Jeffrey believes that life should be wonderful.

In half-light, we see two men making love, and then:

JEFFREY.   Ooh! Oh, oh, I'm sorry!
MAN #1.   What?
JEFFREY.   It broke. *(The lights come up fully on Jeffrey and Man #1 in bed, C.)*
MAN #1.   *(Panicking.)* It broke?
JEFFREY.   *(Reassuring.)* Don't worry.
MAN #1.   It broke?
JEFFREY.   It's okay.

---

* See Special Note on Songs and Recordings on copyright page.

MAN #1. It broke?

JEFFREY. Do you have another?

MAN #1. On the table — the wicker basket.

JEFFREY. *(Looking in the wicker basket.)* It's empty.

MAN #1. Don't you …?

JEFFREY. That was my last one. What should we do? *(Man #1 turns away but remains in bed. Man #2 pops up in bed. The full cast will gradually emerge from the bed, in the manner of clowns piling out of a tiny circus car. Their route of entry will be disguised by the bed's sheets and blankets. As each actor appears, he or she will remain in the bed, which will become quite crowded. Man #2 has a too-sincere, gooey personality.)*

MAN #2. Let's just cuddle.

JEFFREY. Cuddle?

MAN #2. Like little bunnies.

JEFFREY. Bunnies?

MAN #2. Or like little babies.

JEFFREY. Babies?

MAN #2. Can we?

JEFFREY. *(Agreeably.)* Well, okay. *(They begin to cuddle.)*

MAN #2. Isn't this better?

JEFFREY. Than what?

MAN #2. Than sex.

JEFFREY. Sure.

MAN #2. I wuv you, Mommy. *(Jeffrey pulls away. Man #3, a hustler, very slick, pops up in bed. He has a smooth, sexy style.)*

MAN #3. Just relax.

JEFFREY. Gee, I've never paid for sex before.

MAN #3. Just tell me what you want. I'll do anything. *(He strokes Jeffrey's face.)* Hey, you're hot. *(Very bored and professional.)* Okay, I am so turned on now. Let's do it all. Let's get wild. Let's burn down the fuckin' house. Just tell me what you want.

JEFFREY. *(Excited.)* I want to have sex!

MAN #3. *(After a beat.)* You're nuts. *(Man #4 pops up in bed. Jeffrey embraces him.)*

MAN #4. Don't you just adore sex?

JEFFREY. I do!

MAN #4. Even nowadays, isn't it just the best thing ever?

JEFFREY. Oh, yeah!

MAN #4. I always have a great time, even with being careful!

JEFFREY. That's incredible!

MAN #4. I just don't like you. *(Man #5 pops up in bed. He is rather imperious.)*

MAN #5. Yes?

JEFFREY. *(Handing him some papers.)* Here's my latest medical report.

MAN #5. *(Inspecting the papers.)* Um-hmm.

JEFFREY. *(Handing over a form.)* And here's the results of my blood test from a month ago.

MAN #5. *(Wary.)* A month ago?

JEFFREY. *(Handing him another form.)* Last week.

MAN #5. Last week?

JEFFREY. *(Handing him still another form.)* This afternoon.

MAN #5. *(As he checks Jeffrey's throat, eyes, and the glands under his jawline.)* Um-hmm. I'll also need the name of your internist, your most recent X-rays, your passport, and a list of all of your previous sexual contacts.

JEFFREY. Well, okay, but isn't that a little extreme?

MAN #5. Do you *want* the apartment? *(Man #6 pops up in bed. His body is heavily draped in Saran Wrap, head to toe. He also wears rubber surgical gloves and a surgical mask.)*

JEFFREY. Are you ready? *(Man #6 nods yes.)* Do you feel safe? *(Man #6 nods yes.)* I'm just going to stand way over here — *way* over here — and maybe I'll ... jerk off. *(Man #6 looks suspicious and makes a warning noise through his surgical mask. Trying to be cooperative.)* Okay! I won't touch myself! Or you! I'm just going to look at you and — have erotic thoughts. I'm wearing eight condoms, and I won't come! I swear! I promise! *(Man #6 nods okay, a bit doubtfully. Very carefully, very soothingly.)* Okay ... here we go ... this is totally safe. I'm just going to look at you, that's right ... one, two, three ... *(Jeffrey turns and looks at Man #6. Man #6 panics and screams through his surgical mask. Jeffrey refuses to give up and speaks eagerly to the group on the bed.)* Can we — ?

MAN #1. No!

JEFFREY.   Oh, but maybe just —
MAN #2.   No!
JEFFREY.   Oh, oh, but how about just under the —
MAN #3.   No!
JEFFREY.   And we'll be really, really careful —
MAN #1 and MAN #6.   No!
JEFFREY.   And we'll stay totally aware at all times —
MAN #4, #5, and #6.   No!
JEFFREY.   But *please* —
ALL THE MEN EXCEPT JEFFREY.   No!
JEFFREY.   But I swear, I promise —
ALL THE MEN EXCEPT JEFFREY.   NO!
JEFFREY.   But just for one tiny little second —
ALL THE MEN EXCEPT JEFFREY.   NO! NO! NO! *(A Woman pops up in bed; she is lovely and soft-spoken, in a silk negligée.)*
WOMAN.   Hi.
ALL THE MEN, INCLUDING JEFFREY.   *(After a beat, a bit shocked.) NO! (Everyone except Jeffrey collapses onto the bed, as if asleep or unconscious.)*
JEFFREY.   Oh my God, oh no, I wonder if maybe it's really happening! You can feel it coming — oh my God, maybe from now on ... *(All the people on the bed rise up.)*
ALL.   NO MORE SEX! *(Jeffrey climbs out of bed. Lights down on the bed and everyone in it. Jeffrey steps forward and begins to get dressed. He speaks to the audience.)*
JEFFREY.   Okay. Confession time. You know those articles, the ones all those right wingers use? The ones that talk about gay men who've had over five thousand sexual partners? Well, compared to me, they're shut-ins. Wallflowers. But I'm not promiscuous. That is such an ugly word. I'm cheap. I *love* sex. I don't know how else to say it. I always have — I always thought that sex was the reason to grow up. I couldn't wait! I didn't! I mean — sex! It's just one of the truly great ideas. I mean, the fact that our bodies have this built-in capacity for joy — it just makes me love God. Yes!

But I want to be politically correct about this. I know it's wrong to say that all gay men are obsessed with sex. Because

10

that's not true. All *human beings* are obsessed with sex. All gay men are obsessed with opera. And it's not the same thing. Because you can have good sex.

Except — what's going on? I mean, you saw. Things are just — not what they should be. Sex is too sacred to be treated this way. Sex wasn't meant to be safe, or negotiated, or fatal. But you know what really did it? This guy. I'm in bed with him, and he starts crying. And he says, "I'm sorry, it's just — this used to be so much fun."

So. Enough. Facts of life. No more sex. Not for me. Done!

And you know what? It's going to be fine. Because I am a naturally cheerful person. And I will find a substitute for sex. Sex Lite. Sex Helper. I Can't Believe It's Not Sex. I will find a great new way to live, and a way to be happy. So — no more. The sexual revolution is over! England won. No sex! No sex. I'm ready! I'm willing! Let's go! *(Lights up on Gym Rat #1. He is working out, wearing a Walkman. We hear the music on his Walkman — hip-hop. Lights up on Gym Rat #2. He is working out, wearing a Walkman. We hear the music on his Walkman — throbbing disco. Lights up on Gym Rat #3. He is working out, wearing a Walkman. We hear the music on his Walkman — soaring grand opera. The Gym Rats will continue their workouts during the following scene. Jeffrey bounds into the gym, wearing workout clothes.)* It's the answer! I'll pour all my physical needs into working out! Endorphins, not hormones! No sex! Just sweat! *(Jeffrey is now standing beside a barbell resting on supports over a workout bench.)* Can I get a spot? *(Steve, a good-looking, extremely sexual man in his thirties, turns around. Steve is a master at outrageous, successful flirtation; he knows what he wants.)*

STEVE.   You got it.

JEFFREY.   Oh my.

STEVE.   *(Referring to the weights.)* How much do you want on?

JEFFREY.   Oh, forty-fives are fine.

STEVE.   I just joined. Do you like it here?

JEFFREY.   Oh yeah, a lot. *(He lowers his voice to a more masculine pitch.)* Yeah.

STEVE.   *(Offering his hand.)* Steve.

JEFFREY. Jeffrey. *(Lowering his voice.)* Jeff.

STEVE. Are you okay?

JEFFREY. Sure. *(He giggles from nervousness.)* I'm sorry, I'm butching it up. I don't know why I'm doing that. I guess it's to seem sexier — you know, more masculine. *(In an exaggeratedly nelly voice.)* This is the way I really sound. *(In his normal voice.)* I'm sorry.

STEVE. No, don't be. We all do that. Change our personalities, to seem ... hotter. I'm doing it right now.

JEFFREY. Are you?

STEVE. Technically, we haven't even met yet. *(Putting out his hand.)* Steve.

JEFFREY. *(Shaking Steve's hand; romance is now clearly in the air.)* Jeffrey.

STEVE. So, do you want to ... do your set?

JEFFREY. Oh. Yes. Sure. *(Jeffrey lies down on the weight bench. Steve spots Jeffrey on the bench press, monitoring the weight. Steve's crotch is now directly over Jeffrey's face.)*

STEVE. Ready?

JEFFREY. Oh yeah. *(Jeffrey starts bench-pressing, as Steve urges him on, rather erotically.)*

STEVE. One ... two ... that's right ... three ... four ... you love it ... five ... six ... one more — come on, you're ready — I'm with you — it's so good — don't stop — get it up — pump it — keep it coming, baby, baby, you're there, you're doing it — go, go, go, owww!!! *(The workouts of all the other Gym Rats are now in sync with Jeffrey and Steve; all of the men have reached a truly orgasmic crescendo. As Jeffrey's set ends, everyone drops his weights onto the floor with a thud. Steve helps Jeffrey lower the barbell back onto the supports. All of the men in the gym, including Jeffrey and Steve, are now panting, exhausted, as if postorgasm. Jeffrey remains lying on the bench.)* Cigarette?

JEFFREY. What?

STEVE. Great set.

JEFFREY. *(Gazing up at Steve's crotch.)* You too.

STEVE. What?

JEFFREY. *(Sitting up.)* I mean, thanks. For the spot.

STEVE. Anytime. You look great.

JEFFREY. Thanks. You look ... terrific.

STEVE. Jeffrey? Jeff?

JEFFREY. Yeah?

STEVE. What would happen ... if I kissed you? Right now?

JEFFREY. What?

STEVE. Do you want to?

JEFFREY. *Steve* ...

STEVE. We could drive this place crazy. Everyone's being so butch. We could probably kill people.

JEFFREY. Steve ...

STEVE. Chickenshit.

JEFFREY. I am not!

STEVE. Then get over here.

JEFFREY. I can't. I have to — *(Steve grabs Jeffrey and kisses him passionately; Jeffrey responds. As the kiss continues, all of the Gym Rats look at Steve and Jeffrey and, in unison, give a sincere schoolgirl sigh of romantic appreciation.)*

GYM RATS. Awww ... *(Jeffrey pulls away.)*

JEFFREY. No! I won't let this happen! No more! I grabbed my stuff and I ran out of there! *(As he runs across the stage and begins to pull on his street clothes.)* I said no sex and I meant it! No backsliding, no loopholes! And I didn't linger in the locker room and tie my shoe five times while he took off his shorts, I didn't admire my knapsack until he got out of the shower, I didn't accidentally have sex with him — oops! — in the steam room! I erased him, from my mind, from every part of my body! Because I am the new Jeffrey, no longer a slave to my libido, to my urges, or to my reputation as the pushover of lower Manhattan. I just left, with a new inner peace, a serenity. I didn't even glance back to see if he was still watching me. *(Jeffrey glances back; Steve is watching him.)* No! I won't! I ran right up the stairs and into the street! *(Mother Teresa enters. She wears her distinctive full-length white sari with striped blue trim. We do not see her face, which will remain completely hidden in the veil of her sari.)* And I see her. Mother Teresa. Near Blockbuster Video. Was it a hallucination? Or was that really her? I read, later on, that she was actually in the neighborhood, having her cataracts removed at St. Vincent's. But

13

was it her? Or just a truly perverse drag queen? A comfortable one? Well, whoever, or whatever, she was, I know an omen when I see one. *(Mother Teresa crosses the stage and exits.)* But what does it mean? What's her message? I guess it's — be good. Behave. But — what's good? Okay. First step. Goodbye. *(Steve exits. Sterling Farrell enters. Sterling is in his thirties or forties; he is superbly regal and beautifully dressed. Sterling is never bitchy or cruel; he adores his life and his friends, and exults in stylishness. Sterling is an ideal host, generous and amusing. He is Jeffrey's best friend.)*

STERLING.   You saw Mother Teresa?

JEFFREY.   I swear. She was standing right there. On Eighth Avenue.

STERLING.   Well, how did she look?

JEFFREY.   I don't know, she was walking. She looked great.

STERLING.   Oh, please. She's had work done. I saw her on CNN, she looked sixty. *(We are now in an elegant men's shop. A Salesman — pure attitude — is waiting on Sterling. He holds up two expensive sweaters; Sterling is trying to decide between them.)* Teal? Or slate?

JEFFREY.   *(As the Salesman indicates the correct choice.)* Teal. *(Sterling tosses one of the sweaters over his shoulders dramatically, like a cape; the sleeves dangle. He turns his body in profile.)*

STERLING.   Can I do this? Or do I look like some sort of gay superhero? *(Sterling continues to drape the sweater, ever more outlandishly.)*

JEFFREY.   Sterling, I think I'm ... giving up sex.

STERLING.   You are? Why?

SALESMAN.   Did I miss an issue of *New York* magazine?

JEFFREY.   I just think it's time. I love sex so much, but everything's gotten too scary. It's too ... overwhelming.

STERLING.   My dear, what you need is a relationship.

JEFFREY.   A relationship?

SALESMAN.   *(Examining Jeffrey's shoes; he snorts.)* Humph. And shoes.

STERLING.   If you had a boyfriend, you could relax. You'd set the rules once and then you'd be fine. That's what Darius and I did, and we've been together for almost two years. *(The*

Salesman helps him into a jacket.) Do you like this? I mean, on me?

JEFFREY. But aren't you incredibly frustrated?

STERLING. Of course. I'm hard to fit.

JEFFREY. About sex!

STERLING. *(As the Salesman fusses with him, straightening the jacket, removing lint, etc.)* Darling, love is more than just sex. I mean, even trolls can have sex. What you need is a boyfriend. Someone to nest with, wake up with, just lie around the beach house with. *(Delicately pushing the Salesman away.)* Sweetheart. Like Darius.

JEFFREY. But Darius is a dancer.

STERLING. Exactly. I said you needed a boyfriend, not a person. I love having a boyfriend. Not having to worry about going out and finding one. Just having someone there, and I mean this in the best possible way, like a wonderful pet that can feed and walk itself. *(Sincerely.)* I mean, I really do love Darius. I love his body, I love his smile, and he has great hands and feet. On some dancers the toes are all smushed, and I mean I would just say "Sorry, Misha, uh-uh, not without socks." And Darius loves me, Lord knows why. *(Handing the jacket to the Salesman.)* Charge.

JEFFREY. How is Darius? Is he back in *Cats?*

STERLING. Of course. He's fine. It was just a reaction to the AZT. They adjusted the dosage. He's great.

JEFFREY. Of course.

STERLING. You think I don't know what I sound like. Of course I know. But I have made a decision. I have always been lucky, all my life. Obviously. And I have simply decided to stay lucky. *N'est-ce pas?*

JEFFREY. And you still have sex?

STERLING. Of course. Safe sex. The best. *(The Salesman hands Sterling a shopping bag with his purchases.)* Thank you. I mean, Jeffrey — it's just sex. *(A blast of raucous music is heard. A slide of a handsome, fairly unclothed man might fill the stage.)*

JEFFREY. Just sex? Just sex? *(Another blast of music, and perhaps more erotic slides. Skip Winkly, a smarmy, upbeat game-show host, appears, in a flashy tuxedo. He is accompanied by a vapid*

Showgirl.)
SKIP.   Hi! I'm Skip Winkly, and welcome to "It's Just Sex!"
— the show where we explore human sexuality and win big
prizes! *(The Showgirl cues canned applause; slides of garish big
prizes might appear. The Salesman, Sterling, and Jeffrey now stand
behind glittery podiums with buzzers. A sign or slide reads, in Vegas-
caliber letters, "It's Just Sex!")*
SALESMAN.   Hi, Skip.
STERLING.   Hey, Skip.
JEFFREY.   Hi!
SKIP.   What a great set of contestants — three gay men!
And now let's play "It's Just Sex!" And remember — each
question may have more than one correct answer. The most
stylish reply wins! *(The Showgirl hands him a card.)* Here we go
— question number one! What seemingly harmless events can
now be fatal if they occur during sex? *(The Salesman, Jeffrey,
and Sterling all hit their buzzers, one after the other.)*
SALESMAN.   A paper cut.
JEFFREY.   Recent dental work.
STERLING.   Fluorescent lighting.
SKIP.   *(Pointing to Sterling, as the Showgirl cues more applause.)*
Yes, for seventy points!
JEFFREY.   I knew that.
SALESMAN.   Is my buzzer working?
SKIP.   We'll find out! Question number two: Who is your
favorite sexual fantasy? *(The Salesman, Jeffrey, and Sterling all hit
their buzzers again, one after the other.)*
SALESMAN.   Denzel Washington!
JEFFREY.   That guy at the gym.
STERLING.   Yoko Ono. *(Everyone stares at Sterling questioningly.
He rolls his eyes at their obtuseness.)* To see the apartment.
SKIP.   *(Pointing to Sterling.)* Yes again, for seventy points!
JEFFREY.   *(Regarding Sterling.)* He was coached before the
show.
SALESMAN.   I have a slow buzzer!
SKIP.   Now, now! It's time for our bonus round, when ev-
erything could change, for five *hundred* points! Yes! Here we
go: Let's say there's a fella who just loves having sex more

than anything. What will happen to him if he suddenly just flat-out dagnabbit *stops? (There is a pause. No one buzzes.)*

SALESMAN. *(At a loss.)* Gee ...

STERLING. *(At a loss.)* Skip ... *(Jeffrey is suddenly afire with inspiration, and he hits his buzzer.)*

SKIP. Yes! Gay Man #2, with that hopeful, deluded look!

JEFFREY. Skip, my answer is this: If the fella stops having sex, he will pour himself into his career. And all that rechanneled energy will create incredible career karma, and he'll be a huge success and fantastically happy!

SKIP. *(Looking off-stage.)* Judges? What do you say? Will his career compensate? *(He listens to the off-stage judges.)* That's absolutely right! *(The music goes crazy, confetti rains down, and frenzied applause is heard. The Showgirl hands Jeffrey a dozen roses and places a rhinestone tiara on his head. Jeffrey is ecstatic.)* Wait! Hold it! Just a minute! Judges? *(He listens.)* They have a question — it's nothing really, just a minor technicality. A soaring career can compensate for no sex, but — just what is your career?

JEFFREY. Well, I'm an actor ... waiter. *(A pause.)*

SKIP. Which means ...

STERLING. *(Stepping out from behind his podium.)* I win! *(The wild music and confetti resume. The Showgirl grabs Jeffrey's roses and tiara and gives them to Sterling. Skip, the Salesman, and the Showgirl all exit. Sterling begins to exit, and then notices the audience. He beams, and gives a gracious royal wave as he walks off-stage. Jeffrey is alone.)*

JEFFREY. Okay, so I'm an unemployed actor. I mean, I'm talented — I think I am. I mean, last week I read for a part, on a TV show! *(A Casting Director appears, very smug and patronizing, seated, holding a clipboard. Jeffrey is now at an audition. He tries to he ingratiating.)* Hi. Jeffrey Calloway.

CASTING DIRECTOR. *(Handing Jeffrey some pages.)* Page 33. Police Officer #2. Remember, there are no small parts. Well, actually, there are. All right. You've just burst in on the evil ghetto drug lord. Action.

JEFFREY. *(Reading from the pages.)* "Hold it right there, Diego! Freeze!"

CASTING DIRECTOR. *(Not happy.)* You're a hero. You mean

17

business. Again. Action.

JEFFREY. *(A bit more intense.)* "Hold it right there, Diego! Freeze!"

CASTING DIRECTOR. You've been hunting him for months. You've finally got him with the goods. But he might have a gun! Action!

JEFFREY. *(More intense.)* "Hold it right there, Diego! Freeze!"

CASTING DIRECTOR. You hate him! More! Action!

JEFFREY. *(Pouring it on.)* "Hold it right there, Diego! Freeze!"

CASTING DIRECTOR. You loathe him! You scorn him! Make me feel it! More! Prime time!

JEFFREY. *(With ultimate fury, his voice squeaking girlishly as he uses both hands to aim an imaginary gun.)* "Hold it right there, Diego! Freeze! Oh, I just hate you!" *(There is a pause.)*

CASTING DIRECTOR. Perhaps you'd like to read for our gay role. It's not a caricature, it's a very full human being.

JEFFREY. Sure. The gay role?

CASTING DIRECTOR. Page 68. The neighbor. *(Lights down on the Casting Director. Jeffrey steps forward and addresses the audience.)*

JEFFREY. I got the part. The gay role. Two lines. It was the first time I'd worked in almost a year. Which is why I am a waiter. *(Another Waiter appears, hands Jeffrey a starched white service jacket, and exits. Jeffrey puts the jacket on.)* A cater waiter, to be exact. I work for various party outfits — you've heard of them. Glorious Food. Sublime Service. Arugula with Attitude. It's actually kind of fun, because I get to go everywhere, with my shiny black shoes and my garment bag. I've been to private homes, museums, tents in Central Park. It's like gay National Guard. *(The other Waiter reappears. He now wears a bandanna at his throat, cowboy-style. He hands Jeffrey a beaded headband with a feather. Jeffrey puts the headband on as the Waiter exits.)* If you're anyone at all, you've ignored me. But I don't mind, because I've tried on your fur. *(Music begins. Lights up on the ballroom of the Waldorf, decorated with hay, pinto-patterned tablecloths, cacti, and gingham for a country-western theme. Chandeliers descend, also draped in gingham. Steve enters; like Jeffrey and the other waiter, he wears the standard cater-waiter uniform of service jacket, black pants, white shirt, and black bow tie. Steve also wears a red cowboy hat, and perhaps a bandanna. Everyone's country-western accessories should appear fairly ridiculous. Jeffrey and Steve spot one another.)*

STEVE.   Kemo sabe?

JEFFREY.   Pardner?

STEVE.   Howdy!

JEFFREY.   Howdy! *(As Jeffrey and Steve greet each other, the Boss enters. He wears a waiter's uniform and an absurdly oversized cowboy hat. He is a barking bully, perhaps with a Jamaican accent.)*

BOSS.   Gentlemen? What do you think you're doing?

JEFFREY.   *(To Steve, as Jeffrey and the Boss exit.)* Roundup! *(Steve takes his place behind a bar, which is draped with a pinto-patterned tablecloth and set with bottles and glassware. During Ann Marwood Bartle's speeches, he freezes in half-light. Lights up on Ann Marwood Bartle. She is a giddy socialite in an elaborate ball gown accessorized with a sequined cowboy hat, fringed gauntlet gloves, and a holster with pistols. Ann is thrilled beyond measure to be the evening's hostess. She should not be played as southern; think Connecticut lockjaw.)*

ANN.   Good evening, everyone. I'm Ann Marwood Bartle. And I'd like to welcome you to Country-Western Nite here at the Waldorf! A Hoe-down for AIDS. Now more than ever we need to combat this terrible disease with funding, education, and gingham. *(She indicates the ribbons on her bodice.)* The red ribbon I wear stands for AIDS awareness. The lavender ribbon is in memory of those who have died. And the diamond spray is a gift of my first husband. And now I'd like to introduce our honorary board of directors at table number one. Hold your applause, please, for Lauren Bacall! Donna Karan! Mr. and Mrs. Henry Kravis! And our very own, the Honorable Mayor Rudolph Guiliani. In the chaps. *(Ann freezes in half-light. Jeffrey enters with a tray.)*

JEFFREY.   I need a vodka rocks with a twist, and two spritzers.

STEVE.   *(As he makes the drinks.)* I was hoping I'd run into you. I wanted to apologize about the other day, at the gym.

I came on a little strong.

JEFFREY. No, you were great. I'm sorry I took off. I was just acting weird. I'm ... an actor.

STEVE. I thought so. Have I seen you in something?

JEFFREY. Well, did you see *Manhattan Precinct* two weeks ago? Near the end of the show? The gay neighbor? *(Doing sincere, TV-style acting.)* "You know, Karen, I have the same problem ... with Bob."

STEVE. You were great! *(The other Waiter enters, disgruntled, in a full-tilt Indian headdress and a beaded breastplate.)*

JEFFREY. *(Indian-style, to the Waiter.)* How.

WAITER. *(Morose.)* Why? *(The Waiter exits.)*

STEVE. *(Handing Jeffrey a drink in a glass shaped like a cowboy boot.)* Here you go.

JEFFREY. So — what do you really do?

STEVE. I'm actually, really — a bartender. I sort of acted and I sort of wrote, but mostly ...

JEFFREY. What?

STEVE. I watch you.

JEFFREY. *(Pleased.)* You do? *(The Waiter reappears.)*

WAITER. He does. *(The Boss appears.)*

BOSS. Spritzers! Table fifteen! *(Jeffrey and the other Waiter begin to exit to opposite sides of the stage. The waiter pauses and speaks to Jeffrey, regarding Steve.)*

WAITER. Nice work, Little Feather.

JEFFREY. Bitch.

WAITER. Squaw. *(The Waiter, Jeffrey, and the Boss exit. Lights up on Ann.)*

ANN. Is everyone ready to kick up their heels and rustle their petticoats for a new outpatient lounge? Cowhands, cowgals, I give you a very special treat! They've been practicing for — weeks! Let's have a big whoop-ti-aye-ay for Dr. Sidney Greenblatt and his Mount Sinai Ramblers! *(A raucous country-western square dance tune begins. Jeffrey enters with an empty tray. He stares at the dance floor.)*

JEFFREY. Oh my God ... *(Ann begins clapping her hands and calling the square dance.)*

ANN. Come on, everyone! Get out on the floor! Here we

go! It's a square dance! Yee-haw!

JEFFREY.   *(To Steve.)* Isn't this bizarre? But I think they're raising a fortune.

STEVE.   You're making small talk.

JEFFREY.   I need a Bloody Mary and two more spritzers.

STEVE.   Am I making you nervous?

JEFFREY.   Yes!

STEVE.   I like you nervous.

JEFFREY.   Why?

STEVE.   I have to tell you something. At the gym — that wasn't the first time I saw you.

JEFFREY.   It wasn't?

STEVE.   No. I've seen you at parties — at the Met, the Armory. You are always chattering away.

JEFFREY.   Oh no.

STEVE.   What?

JEFFREY.   I have this image of myself as ... a normal person — you know, a guy. But I've always known that I'm secretly really ... a teenage girl.

STEVE.   No! You're great! You're a great teenage girl! The other waiters, they're moody, they're Brando. But you — you have a ball. You belong at the party.

JEFFREY.   So do you. *(The Waiter appears in his headdress with a tray.)*

WAITER.   *(À la* Poltergeist.*)* He's baaack ... *(The Boss enters, very angry.)*

BOSS.   What is this, a social club? Do you want to be fired?

WAITER.   I want my land.

BOSS.   Move! *(The Waiter and Jeffrey exit, followed by the Boss.)*

ANN.   C'mon, y'all! *(Calling the square dance.)* Swing your partners, round you go, allemande left, then do-si-do! *(Speaking normally.)* Isn't this fun? You little dogies! *(Jeffrey enters with an empty tray.)*

STEVE.   So have we talked enough? Can I see you? After the party?

JEFFREY.   I need two glasses of champagne.

STEVE.   California?

JEFFREY.   No — the good stuff. *(Steve starts to pour two glasses*

of champagne.)
STEVE.   Do you have a lover?
JEFFREY.   No.
STEVE.   Are you seeing someone?
JEFFREY.   No.
STEVE.   Do I care?
JEFFREY.   You are unbelievable!
STEVE.   Find out. *(He laughs.)* I'm sorry, I keep hitting on you. Don't you love this part?
JEFFREY.   What part?
STEVE.   The part where you can't find out enough, about the other person. Where it's all interesting, where it all seems ... sexy. First steps.
JEFFREY.   To where?
STEVE.   To my place. Or your place. Or happiness. Or ... more.
JEFFREY.   You move fast.
STEVE.   Catch up. Because if I don't touch you very soon, I may explode.
JEFFREY.   You know, until about a minute ago, I had a very strong reason not to go out with you.
STEVE.   Which was? No, wait — is it because ... I'm a cowboy, and you're ... a waiter?
JEFFREY.   We're a proud people.
STEVE.   What a shame.
JEFFREY.   *(Toasting Steve with the champagne.)* You know, in a better world, I could ask you to square dance.
STEVE.   Really? You want to square dance? *(Steve holds up his hand. He looks at Ann Marwood Bartle.)*
ANN.   Bow to your partner, then once more ... *(Steve snaps his fingers.)* Cater waiters, take the floor! *(The lights grow brighter. Steve steps out from behind the bar. He bows to Jeffrey and holds out his hand. Jeffrey takes Steve's hand and they begin to dance a rousing, sexy two-step, the Cotton-Eyed Joe. As Steve and Jeffrey dance, the Waiter and the Boss appear and begin to dance as well, as a couple. Ann Marwood Bartle joins the number; she might hold a hobbyhorse or fire her pistols. The number becomes a spirited, miniature version of a real Busby Berkeley hoe-down complete with square*

dancing and "Yee-haw!"'s. As the number grows in wildness, Steve begins to remove Jeffrey's clothing; he tosses the discarded items to the other people on stage. Jeffrey's headband comes off, and then his jacket; everyone surrounds Jeffrey and begins to caress him. Jeffrey pulls away from Steve and the group.)

JEFFREY. No! (The music stops abruptly, and Ann, the Waiter, and the Boss exit.)

STEVE. You can't do that. This is my fantasy.

JEFFREY. (Very torn.) I have to circulate. Table 22.

STEVE. Come on — one more do-si-do.

JEFFREY. I'm working!

STEVE. What is going on with you?

JEFFREY. (Very distraught.) We're not allowed to have fantasies! Not anymore!

STEVE. Come on. Let's go.

JEFFREY. I can't!

STEVE. Why not?

JEFFREY. It's ... I can't explain! It's not you! Yes, it is you!

STEVE. What?

JEFFREY. I have to go! (Steve and the hoe-down vanish. As they do, Sterling enters, wearing something outrageous, perhaps Chinese-inspired lounging pajamas.)

STERLING. So — he was really cute, this bartender? (We are now in Sterling's elegant, if somewhat overdone, Upper East Side apartment. Sterling holds a cigarette and a cocktail.)

JEFFREY. He was fantastic. But I just got so — I don't know! I went nuts!

STERLING. Jeffrey — you are beginning to have a problem. (Darius, Sterling's boyfriend, enters, wearing an overcoat. Darius is a true innocent, a handsome, completely sweet dancer in his twenties.)

DARIUS. Hi, guys.

STERLING. Hello, sweetheart.

DARIUS. What a day. I am exhausted. (Darius takes off his coat. He is wearing his costume from Cats, which consists of a heavily painted body suit, accentuated with yarn and fur, elaborate leg warmers, knitted gauntlets, and a tail. He has already removed his makeup.)

JEFFREY. Darius — aren't you supposed to leave your costume at the theater?

DARIUS.   We were filming a commercial, the new one, and it went late. I got stuck. So you're not having sex anymore. *(Darius sits beside Sterling; they are very easy and affectionate with one another. Their love affair is real and lasting. The friendship between Jeffrey, Sterling, and Darius should also be one of great pleasure and devotion.)*

STERLING.   What he needs is to fall in love and have a relationship. And then this sex thing will fall into place.

DARIUS.   Exactly. Look at us. Look at how happy we are. Don't we make you want to fall in love?

STERLING.   You know, sometimes I think we should be on a brochure for Middle America. So that everyone can say, "Oh, look, a wholesome gay couple!"

JEFFREY.   Excuse me? You're not wholesome. You're a decorator — excuse me, an interior designer — there, I said it without giggling. And you — you're a dancer. You two are like Martha Stewart and Ann Miller. Which, believe me, I prefer. I hate that gay role models are supposed to be just like straight people. As if straight people were even like that.

STERLING.   That's true. I was watching these two guys on *Nightline,* on Gay Pride Day? And one of them said, "I'm Bob Wheeler and I'm a surgeon. And my lover is an attorney. And we'd like to show America that all gays aren't limp-wristed, screaming queens. There are gay truck drivers and gay cops and gay lumberjacks." And I just thought, "Ooh — get *her.*"

DARIUS.   Who's Martha Stewart?

STERLING.   She writes picture books about gracious living. Martha says that nothing else matters, if you can do a nice dried floral arrangement. I worship her.

DARIUS.   And who's Ann Miller?

STERLING.   Leave this house. *(Jeffrey and Sterling freeze. Darius addresses the audience.)*

DARIUS.   Some people think I'm dumb, just because I'm a chorus boy with an eighth-grade education. Well — I live in a penthouse and I don't pay rent. I go to screenings and I take cabs. Dumb, huh? And yes, I'm in *Cats.* Now and forever. And I love it! I do! I figure I was too young for *A Chorus*

Line, and too happy for *Les Miz.* I never got that show — *Les Miz.* It's about this French guy, right, who steals a loaf of bread, and then he suffers for the rest of his life. For *toast.* Get over it! *(Back to the scene.)*

JEFFREY.   That's why I came over. To be convinced about this love-and-relationship bit. Because I do believe that you two are truly in love. You have that special ... smugness. You're like an advertisement for connubial bliss.

DARIUS.   What's "connubial"?

STERLING.   It's when one of us can afford a cleaning woman. *(The doorbell rings. Steve enters, carrying a bouquet of flowers.)* Steven! Hi!

DARIUS.   What a surprise!

JEFFREY.   Oh my God ...

STERLING.   Jeffrey, this is Steven. I met him at the showhouse opening, and we talked.

DARIUS.   We love him.

STEVE.   *(Handing Jeffrey the flowers.)* Hi there.

JEFFREY.   How are you?

STERLING.   I think they're perfect for each other.

DARIUS.   Me too.

STERLING.   Steve's a bartender, so they'll have something in common. They can fall in love and cater together — it'll be like *Roots.*

JEFFREY.   *(To Steve, with great, accelerating passion.)* Steve — since the first second I saw you, at the gym, I have thought of nothing and no one else. I have fantasized about you — naked — about you kissing me and talking to me and walking down the street with me, and letting you do things to me that I have only permitted with five thousand other men. I think you could change my life and change the world and I would love more than anything to do exactly the same for you and I think it's completely and totally possible that we could be the happiest people alive except — I'm not having sex anymore so — sorry! *(Jeffrey, in agony, hands the flowers back to Steve and collapses into a chair.)*

STERLING.   Wait — you two already know each other.

STEVE.   We do.

DARIUS.   Oh my God. Oh my God. *(To Sterling.)* It's like I told you. I'm psychic — I can predict boyfriends!

JEFFREY.   We're not boyfriends! *(Steve, Sterling, and Darius surround Jeffrey, standing or kneeling around his chair.)*

STEVE.   Jeffrey, calm down. Stop hyperventilating.

JEFFREY.   I can't!

STEVE.   Take a deep breath. *(As conducted by Sterling, all four men take a deep breath.)* Better?

JEFFREY.   Sort of.

STEVE.   Okay. Now, I want to see you. We can take this as slow as you like. First step. How about — tomorrow night?

JEFFREY.   I'm working! Till ten!

STEVE.   Afterwards. We'll have dinner.

STERLING.   *(To Jeffrey.)* You must.

DARIUS.   You can't ignore the karma. It's too dangerous.

STERLING.   You have to get over this bizarre sex thing.

DARIUS.   You'll have fun! You'll have appetizers!

STERLING.   We're your friends.

DARIUS.   We love you.

STERLING.   You must obey us.

STEVE.   You have no choice, Jeffrey. Dinner?

STERLING.   *(To Jeffrey.)* Dinner?

DARIUS.   *(To Jeffrey.)* Dinner?

JEFFREY.   Well …

DARIUS.   Oh, come on. You're gay. You're single.

STERLING.   It isn't pretty.

JEFFREY.   Yes! *(Sterling, Darius, and Steve cheer.)*

STERLING.   *(Hugging Jeffrey.)* I'm so proud of you! You're dating again!

STEVE.   How about the Paris Commune? On Bleecker? I know the maître d'.

JEFFREY.   Yes!

STEVE.   And Jeffrey?

JEFFREY.   Yes?

STEVE.   I just … okay, just so there are no surprises …

JEFFREY.   Uh-huh.

STEVE.   I'm HIV-positive.

JEFFREY.   *(After a beat.)* Um, okay, right.

STEVE. Does that make a difference?

JEFFREY. No. No. Of course not.

STERLING. *(Dismissing any doubt.)* Please.

DARIUS. HIV-positive men are the hottest.

STEVE. I mean — I'd understand. I'd be hurt and disappointed, but — I just wanted to be clear.

JEFFREY. No, really, it's fine — I mean, come on, it's the nineties, right? The Paris Commune, at ten. I can't wait.

DEBRA. *(Entering from the rear of the theater.)* Do you feel lost? *(Lights down on Steve, Sterling, Darius, and the apartment. Jeffrey steps forward.)*

JEFFREY. I do! *(Debra is an attractive, vibrant, magnetic woman in a stylish Armani suit. She is in turn ferocious, deeply compassionate, abusive, and a red-hot mama. She is the evangelist as pop star, capable of seducing and threatening her audience — she is the most confident person on earth.)*

DEBRA. *(Approaching the stage.)* So you come to me, and you say, "Debra, what can I do to feel better about myself and the world?," and you know what I say?

JEFFREY. What?

DEBRA. Love. It's real. It works. Go for it!

JEFFREY. *(To the audience.)* Debra Moorhouse — the nation's hottest postmodern evangelist. *(Jeffrey leaves the stage to watch from the audience. Debra picks up a microphone and begins to work the crowd — she will use the actual theatergoers as her flock.)*

DEBRA. I'm not here as a priest, or a guru, or as any sort of religious leader. I'm just someone who — likes to talk. And people come to me, and they say, "Debra, I'm in love with an alcoholic, what should I do?" And I tell them, "Don't look to me for answers — look to yourself. And then turn it all over to some higher power, whether that power is simply the collective strength of all the love in the world, or some dude named — Jesus Christ. *(She offers a nod and a salute to heaven.)* Find that source of unconditional love, find that all-encompassing, ultimate love, surrender to that unending, infinite love that will let you say, 'Hey *(Her voice shifts from cajoling to a harsh bellow)* — FUCK YOU! Get out of my house until you stop drinking!'" *(She smiles radiantly.)* Let's have some ques-

tions. Yes? *(Various trembling, sincere followers raise their hands, yearning for Debra's attention. Debra points to a lucky male Acolyte.)*
ACOLYTE #1.   Um, Debra, first of all, I just want to thank you for speaking to us tonight ...
DEBRA.   You bet. What's up?
ACOLYTE #1.   Well, um, I just broke up with my lover.
DEBRA.   Well, we've all been there, haven't we?
ACOLYTE #1.   *(Puzzled.)* With my lover?
DEBRA.   Spill, baby.
ACOLYTE #1.   *(As Debra holds out the microphone.)* Well, Brad and I have lived together for almost five years, but then he lost his job and started doing cocaine. And he wouldn't look for work and I was paying for everything and we would have these terrible fights and ... he even tried to hit me with the car. *My* car.
DEBRA.   Whoa. Man.
ACOLYTE #1.   But I still love him!
DEBRA.   *(Almost laughing, looking at Acolyte #1 as if he's crazy.)* Okay. Okay. Let me cook on this! Okay. Okay. *(Serious again.)* It sounds like you've got a problem with everybody's favorite — low self-esteem. Of course, I don't know you. Maybe you *should* have low self-esteem.
ACOLYTE #1.   I just want a relationship.
DEBRA.   You want a relationship because you're afraid! It all goes back to mother, doesn't it? Did you love your mother?
ACOLYTE #1.   Well, I guess so ...
DEBRA.   Don't lie to me. I'll call her. Did she withhold? Was there ... abuse?
ACOLYTE #1.   *(Choked up.)* Sometimes ...
DEBRA.   Go see her. Tell her, "Mom, you were chilly." *(Acolyte #1 bursts into sobs; Debra takes him in her arms.)* "You forgot my birthday. You beat me with a baseball bat. But I understand. I forgive. I *love* you. And Mom, now you're old. You've got a plastic hip. *(Triumphantly.)* And I've got the bat!" *(She pushes Acolyte #1 away.)* Next?
ACOLYTE #2.   Debra, Debra, Debra!!! *(Acolyte #2, another man, is wildly overemotional; he leaps onto the stage.)* First of all, I want to say that I listen to your audiocassettes at least eight times

a day, even in the car on my way to and from work.

DEBRA. Good.

ACOLYTE #2. I've memorized most of them, and sometimes I recite right along with you. *(Debra makes a gesture "And?")* I used to be afraid all the time, but you've really helped me to have a life!

DEBRA. *You've* helped you to have a life. *(Acolyte #2 smacks his forehead in recognition of this great truth. He pulls a pair of hand-crocheted baby booties out of his pocket.)*

ACOLYTE #2. And I just wanted to give you this pair of booties that I hand-crocheted for your baby. I know you discourage gifts, except donations, but — I just had to! *(Acolyte #2 hands Debra the booties. Overcome, he gives her a big wet kiss on the cheek and bounces off the stage. Debra surreptitiously wipes her cheek with the booties.)*

DEBRA. Well, thank you! These are adorable. But remember, I'm not your idol, your Elvis. Don't worship me — *love* me! Do you see the difference?

ACOLYTE #2. Yeah, okay!

DEBRA. One more!

JEFFREY. Hi, Debra. Debra, I think that sex is the best thing ever, but I've met someone, and he's HIV-positive, and I'm beginning to self-destruct. Now, I'm a waiter, so I can't afford your cassettes, or the mug, or the calendar. Do they mention this problem?

DEBRA. They sure do. It's in my book, chapter ten — cheap waiters! *(She laughs at her joke, then grows serious.)* No, no, no. What you're talking about is evil, am I right? Why is there disease? Why was there a Hitler? *(She holds up the booties.)* Why are these acrylic? Ha! Isn't laughter the best medicine? *(Acolyte #2 gives a half-hearted laugh; Debra dismisses him.)* Anyway. Here's the lowdown on evil: it's the absence of love. Ta-da. That's it. Case closed. Where you don't have love, illness makes a home.

JEFFREY. Wait, Debra — are you saying that people get sick because they don't love enough, or because no one loves them?

DEBRA.   It may sound simplistic, it may sound cruel, it may sound like I am blaming people for their own illness, and maybe I am. *(Perky again.)* That's Debra!

JEFFREY.   Debra, that's crazy.

DEBRA.   Think about it! That's it! I'd like to end tonight's session with five minutes of guided meditation. First, I'd like everyone to take the hands of the people on either side of you. *(Jeffrey holds hands in between Acolyte #1 and Acolyte #2.)* Close your eyes. Close 'em up. I'd like you to picture yourself as a very young child. You're four or five, you're innocent, open to love. For maybe the last time in your life, you're very appealing. Can you see that child?

ACOLYTE #1.   I see him!

ACOLYTE #2.   I see him!

DEBRA.   *(To Jeffrey.)* What about you, Mr. I'm-on-a-Budget?

JEFFREY.   I ... I think I see him.

DEBRA.   Give him a kiss! Take that child in your arms! Hug him! Squeeze him! Tickle him till he can't breathe and the eyes roll back in his head! Now tell him — "I love you!"

ACOLYTE #1, ACOLYTE #2, and JEFFREY.   I love you!

DEBRA.   I can't hear you!

ACOLYTE #1, ACOLYTE #2, and JEFFREY.   *(Louder.)* I LOVE YOU!

DEBRA.   Make him believe it!

ACOLYTE #1, ACOLYTE #2, and JEFFREY.   *(As passionately as possible, howling.)* I LOVE YOU!!!

DEBRA.   *(She can't resist.)* Debra!

ACOLYTE #1, ACOLYTE #2, and JEFFREY.   DEBRA!!!

DEBRA.   *(Suspensefully.)* Next week's topic: Dead-end job? Dead-end marriage? Dead-end life? *(Ferociously.)* Stop whining, you big baby! *(With a wave and a smile.)* 'Night! *(Lights down on Debra and her acolytes. We hear a phone ring.)*

STEVE'S VOICE.   *(On his answering machine.)* Hi, this is Steve. I'm not in right now. Please leave a message after the beep. Have a great day.

JEFFREY.   *(To the audience.)* I'm sorry.

JEFFREY'S VOICE.   *(On Steve's answering machine.)* Steve, hi, it's Jeffrey. And ... I'm working later than I thought. Private party, you know. So can we reschedule? Next week? Maybe? I ... I can't wait, and I'll call you, and ... I ... take care.

JEFFREY. *(To the audience.)* I know what you're thinking. What a sleazoid, what a major-league, hall-of-fame rat. And maybe you're right. It's just ... okay, what am I so afraid of? Him getting sick? Me getting sick? Why is the idea of a simple dinner now like an evening of Russian roulette? And I felt like a complete creep, and I couldn't go home and be alone with myself, and I was so horny. Why is that my response to everything? *(Lights up on a shirtless, well-built Man in a leather biker's jacket and a jockstrap.)*

MAN IN JOCKSTRAP. Hey.

JEFFREY. Why can't I drink? *(Lights up on another man, in leather chaps and a harness. He speaks in a deep, practiced, ridiculously sexual basso.)*

MAN IN CHAPS. Uh-huh.

JEFFREY. And if I can't touch anyone else, who can I touch? *(Lights up on Don, a tough guy wearing a leather vest over his bare chest, a leather top man's cap, and Levi's.)*

DON. Welcome — to the Lower Manhattan Gentlemen's Masturbation Society. Or, as we call it in our brochure, Beats All. I'm Don, tonight's sergeant-at-arms. Anyone not following our basic guidelines will be asked to leave and, if necessary, ejected. There will be no bodily contact, and no exchange of fluids. Please feel free to remove as much clothing as you like. We are into hot men, mutual getting off, and masculine appreciation. *(We hear the sounds of a heavy iron door slamming shut and locks turning.)* The doors have been locked, and we think it's going to be a very hot night. *(The Men are now standing in separate down lights; the atmosphere is very rough and shadowy. As they speak, in their lowest, huskiest, most seductive voices, the Men pinch, rub, and slap various parts of their bodies. Jeffrey stands in the center of the group a bit D. The other Men eye him.)*

MAN IN JOCKSTRAP. Hey.

DON. Hey.

MAN IN CHAPS. Hey.

JEFFREY. *(Pleasantly.)* Hey.

MAN IN JOCKSTRAP. Hot bod, man.

DON. Real hot.

MAN IN CHAPS. Uh-huh.

JEFFREY. Okay ...

MAN IN JOCKSTRAP. Nice tits, man.

DON. Hot tits.

MAN IN CHAPS. Uh-huh.

JEFFREY. *(Starting to rub his chest, tentatively.)* Hot.

DON. Nice butt, man.

MAN IN JOCKSTRAP. Hot fuckin' *butt.*

MAN IN CHAPS. Uh-huh.

JEFFREY. Thank you.

MAN IN JOCKSTRAP. Hot *bubble* butt.

JEFFREY. Thank you very much.

DON. I want to see you touch that butt.

MAN IN JOCKSTRAP. Touch that hot butt.

MAN IN CHAPS. Uh-huh.

JEFFREY. Okay ... *(The Man In Chaps has started to slap his own butt with both hands. Jeffrey starts to rub his own butt.)*

DON. That's right.

MAN IN JOCKSTRAP. Hot fuckin' butt!

MAN IN CHAPS. Uh-huh.

JEFFREY. *(Growling.)* Yeah ... *(Everyone but Jeffrey begins to rub his own crotch.)*

MAN IN JOCKSTRAP. Do it, man.

DON. Touch that dick.

MAN IN CHAPS. Uh-huh.

JEFFREY. Touch it? *(Jeffrey begins to rub his own crotch. He continues to rub his butt with his other hand.)*

DON. That's right.

MAN IN JOCKSTRAP. Go for it, man!

MAN IN CHAPS. Uh-huh.

JEFFREY. *(As he rubs his crotch and his butt.)* Why do I feel like — I'm on the subway? This isn't working, not for me. I wonder if I can just kind of ... slip out ... *(Jeffrey stops rubbing himself. He tries to leave. The other Men do not approve.)*

DON, MAN IN JOCKSTRAP, MAN IN CHAPS. *(Very threatening.)* UH-UH! *(The other Men begin to encircle Jeffrey, coming closer and closer.)*

JEFFREY. Oh my God ...
DON. Take 'em down!
JEFFREY. What?
MAN IN JOCKSTRAP. Let's see that butt!
JEFFREY. Guys ...
DON. Come on, man!
MAN IN JOCKSTRAP. Here we go! Take 'em down! Rip 'em down!
DON. Gettin' hot!
MAN IN CHAPS. Uh-huh! *(As the Men begin to unbutton their jeans, we hear a shrill blast on a whistle. Everyone freezes.)*
STERLING. Stop that!
DARIUS. Leave him alone! *(Sterling and Darius have entered, wearing black T-shirts with huge pink paw prints on them. They also wear pink berets and silver whistles on thongs around their necks. They confront the men from the masturbation club, who scamper away. The lights grow bright again.)*
STERLING. We are the Pink Panthers! *(Sterling and Darius strike a dramatic pose as conquering heroes.)*
JEFFREY. *(Very entertained.)* You are?
STERLING. We just got off our shift. We're part of a citizens' patrol to prevent gay bashing. We patrolled with five other guys, from Christopher to Bank Street.
DARIUS. From Seventh Avenue to the river. And we have whistles, and walkie-talkies. *(Sterling displays his walkie-talkie as if it were in a showroom.)*
JEFFREY. I'm so impressed!
STERLING. We're keeping the streets safe. It was Darius's idea.
DARIUS. I wanted to do something.
STERLING. Something with a T-shirt. Don't you love it? *(Sterling and Darius twirl and pose, modeling their T-shirts with great flair.)* I'm sorry, those students in Tiananmen Square were very misguided. Where were the graphics? All it would've taken was one silk-screen. Mao with a *Ghostbusters* circle. *(He demonstrates the circle with a line through it, on his chest.)*
DARIUS. Or that *Miss Saigon* doodle.
STERLING. We heart cultural freedom.

DARIUS. *(Admiring his T-shirt.)* These are going to be very rare. We have to change our name.

JEFFREY. Why?

STERLING. MGM has started a lawsuit. They own the rights to all the *Pink Panther* movies and they claim it's a copyright infringement.

DARIUS. Even though we are a non ...

STERLING and DARIUS. *(Sterling helps Darius with the phrase.)* Profit ...

DARIUS. ... organization to prevent violence.

STERLING. They claim it's not homophobia, but you know it is. So we're testing all the other studios. We've come up with a great new name for our patrol.

JEFFREY. What?

STERLING. Fantasia.

DARIUS. So how was your date? Where's Steve?

JEFFREY. He ... I had to cancel. I just got off work.

DARIUS. Did you call him?

JEFFREY. Of course. I left a message on his machine.

DARIUS. Left a message? Call him again! He's a doll! *(The beeper on Sterling's walkie-talkie goes off.)*

STERLING. *(Into his walkie-talkie, in a very butch voice.)* Hello. Pink Panthers. *(More social.)* Oh, hello, darling.

DARIUS. Is someone in trouble?

STERLING. *(Listening to the walkie-talkie, very upset.)* Really ... No ... Oh no.

JEFFREY. What?

STERLING. We have to get over to Washington Square right away. It's Todd, that huge bodybuilder from the gym!

DARIUS. Oh, no. Not Todd!

STERLING. In shorts! *(Sterling and Darius blow their whistles and exit at a gallop. Jeffrey watches them go. Steve enters from the opposite side of the stage.)*

STEVE. Jeffrey.

JEFFREY. Steve! Did you —?

STEVE. I got your message. That party. You poor guy. But I was all revved up, so I went out anyway. Dancing.

JEFFREY. Great. I … I …
STEVE. I know.
JEFFREY. No, I really …
STEVE. Jeffrey, it's not the first time this has happened to me. You freaked. Cold feet.
JEFFREY. That's not true …
STEVE. Stop it. I can understand, about the HIV thing. It's not easy. But I don't like lying about it. I don't like … politeness. Not anymore.
JEFFREY. I'm sorry. I just — couldn't deal with it. Not right now.
STEVE. Okay. Fine. *(A beat.)* There's lots of things we could do. Safe things. Hot things.
JEFFREY. I know …
STEVE. But you just … don't want to.
JEFFREY. I'm sorry.
STEVE. You're sorry. I'm sorry. It's the new national anthem. You said that you … thought about me. That you … fantasized.
JEFFREY. I know.
STEVE. Do you? Still?
JEFFREY. *(After a beat.)* Yes.
STEVE. But … Jesus Christ. Jesus *Christ.* I can take being sick, I can fucking take dying, but I can't take this.
JEFFREY. You should have told me.
STEVE. I did.
JEFFREY. Sooner! Before … things happened!
STEVE. Before I kissed you!
JEFFREY. Yes!
STEVE. Okay! You didn't have all the … information. Okay. I've been positive for almost five years. I was sick once, my T-cells are decent, and every once in a while, like fifty times a day — an hour — I get very tired of being a person with AIDS. A red ribbon. So sometimes … I forget. Sometimes I choose to forget. Sometimes I choose to be a gay man with a dick. Can you understand? At all?
JEFFREY. Yes.

STEVE. Can I ... forget again?

JEFFREY. No.

STEVE. Can I do something, say something, that will let this happen? I want you, Jeffrey. I may very well even love you. And that means nothing? That should beat anything. That should win!

JEFFREY. I know.

STEVE. Then why are you the one with the problem? Why do I get to be both sick and begging? *(A beat.)* Why won't you kiss me? *(Jeffrey moves toward Steve. They are about to kiss. Jeffrey pulls away.)*

JEFFREY. I'm sorry — no, I'm sorry I said I'm sorry! I'm sorry you're sick! And I'm sorry I lied! I'm sorry it's not ten years ago, and I'm sorry that life is suddenly ... radioactive!

STEVE. *(After a beat, staring at Jeffrey.)* Apology accepted. *(Steve exits.)*

JEFFREY. *(Exploding.)* I hate sex! I hate love! I hate the world for giving me everything, and then taking it all back! *(Two Thugs appear from the shadows on either side of Jeffrey.)*

THUG #1. What's up?

JEFFREY. *(Unsure.)* Hey.

THUG #2. Are you ... gay?

JEFFREY. *(After a beat.)* Mom?

THUG #1. You a faggot?

JEFFREY. Yes.

THUG #2. You queer?

JEFFREY. Please — don't do this.

THUG #1. Suck my dick.

JEFFREY. Do you really want me to do that?

THUG #1. Yeah. No!

THUG #2. Fuck you, man.

JEFFREY. Look, why are you doing this? On Christopher Street?

THUG #1. What is this, like, sacred ground?

JEFFREY. Maybe.

THUG #1. You think you're so special? What are you, one of them fancy faggots? You go to the gym, you got nice friends, you think you're so hot?

JEFFREY. No.

THUG #2. You think you're better than us?

JEFFREY. I'm a waiter.

THUG #1. A waiter? Like at a restaurant?

JEFFREY. Sort of.

THUG #1. They let you touch food? Put your faggoty fingers on it?

JEFFREY. Yes they do. I touch it all the time. I spit in it.

THUG #2. Jesus. What restaurant?

JEFFREY. (Sizing up the Thugs.) Pizza Hut.

THUGS #1 and #2. (Very grossed out.) Uck! Damn! Shit!

THUG #1. Let's dust his ass.

JEFFREY. Fine. Kill me. You're the ones who'll suffer. The rest of your lives. Buffet style.

THUG #2. Shut the fuck up.

JEFFREY. You have weapons. So do I.

THUG #1. I got a knife. What do you got?

JEFFREY. Irony. Adjectives. Eyebrows.

THUG #2. Fuck you. Hold him! (Thug #1 holds Jeffrey while Thug #2 punches him in the stomach. Jeffrey doubles over in pain. The Thugs throw Jeffrey onto the ground and kick him. One Thug holds Jeffrey's arms while the other goes through Jeffrey's pockets.) Shit.

THUG #1. (Digging in Jeffrey's pocket.) He's got cash! (They hear a distant siren. As the Thugs panic, Jeffrey bites the leg of Thug #2.)

THUG #2. Shit, he's bitin' my leg! I'm gonna get AIDS! (The siren grows louder.)

THUG #1. Come on! (Thug #2 gives Jeffrey one more, particularly vicious kick. The two Thugs run off. Jeffrey moans. He struggles to sit up.)

JEFFREY. Shit. Owww. (Mother Teresa enters. She kneels beside Jeffrey, cradling him.) Terry. (Mother Teresa strokes him.) Oww. (To Mother Teresa.) You know, when that asshole started kicking me, I had this horrible stupid thought, this flash, that at least it was ... physical contact. Well, I think I've found my substitute for sex. A substitute for everything. Bruises. Phone ma-

chines. Fear. *(Mother Teresa takes Jeffrey's hand. Jeffrey looks up at the night sky. He looks at Mother Teresa. He begins to sing, a bit of the Gershwins' "Nice Work If You Can Get It."*)*
Holding hands at midnight
'Neath a starry sky
Nice work if you can get it
And you can get it if you try
Loving one who loves you
And then taking that vow
Nice work if you can get it
And if you get it
Won't you tell me … how …
(The lights fade.)

*   See Special Note on Music copyright page.

ACT TWO

A slide sign appears, reading "Sexual Compulsives Anonymous."

There is a microphone on a stand at center stage. A Man enters and moves to the microphone.

TIM. Hi. My name is Tim, and I am a sexual compulsive.
CHORUS OF OFFSTAGE VOICES. HI, TIM!
TIM. Today I have already performed oral sex on three different people. I can't help myself. I'm an agent. *(Tim leaves the stage. Sharon enters, a clearly depressed woman. She stands at the microphone.)*
SHARON. *(With great difficulty.)* Hi. My name is Sharon, and I ... I'm a sexual compulsive.
CHORUS OF OFFSTAGE VOICES. HI, SHARON!
SHARON. Oh, that felt good. *(She takes a deep breath.)* I feel like ... I'm on my way. Admitting I have a problem is the first step to healing. *(Unconsciously, she begins to stroke the microphone stand, up and down, with her hand.)* Now, for the first time in my life, I feel like I don't need a man to define myself. *(She notices a guy in the front row.)* Hi there. *(Sharon, very frustrated, leaves the stage. Dave enters and stands at the microphone.)*
DAVE. Hi. My name is Dave, and I'm sexually compulsive.
CHORUS OF OFFSTAGE VOICES. HI, DAVE!
DAVE. I just love sex. Maybe it's because I have a constant erection, twenty-four hours a day. Or because my penis is fourteen inches long.
CHORUS OF OFFSTAGE VOICES. *(Very interested.)* Oooh. Hi, Dave. *(Sharon reappears, staring at Dave, completely smitten. He nods his head, and she follows him off-stage. As they exit, Jeffrey enters and stands at the microphone.)*
JEFFREY. Hi. My name is Jeffrey, and I'm ... just like you.
CHORUS OF OFFSTAGE VOICES. Jeffrey ...

JEFFREY. I'm a sexual compulsive. But I haven't had sex in almost six months! *(Applause from off-stage.)* I never even think about sex, not anymore. And I used to ... be compulsive. *(More applause and cheers.)* All because of Billy Kearny. I blame him! That's where it started. He kept daring me. "I dare you to take off your clothes — even your underpants." "I dare you to kiss me — on the mouth." Oh God. Two naked fourteen-year-old boys, in front of the big mirror in my parents' bedroom. I'm having sex. And I'm watching myself have sex. Please don't do that. Please don't stop. *(Jeffrey's memory has become very alive and emotional.)* Stop. *(Lights up on the full stage. Jeffrey is wearing his waiter's uniform. He takes his place behind a long rectangular table covered with a floral chintz tablecloth. There is a silver chafing dish on the table, along with china and linen napkins. To the audience.)* I'm working. A memorial. Another one. At a townhouse. It's for a curator, at the Met. The speakers are great. His straight brother. His doctor. His gorgeous Italian boyfriend. *(Jeffrey smiles at the boyfriend, across the room.)* Oh, my God, I am so disgusting. Do you know what I'm doing? I'm cruising a memorial. *(Sterling enters, in a stylish black suit, with a cocktail.)*
STERLING. Oh, please — everybody is. That boyfriend. Carlo. I'm telling you, while Jessye Norman was singing that hymn, everyone was watching *that* him. It's not that we're not sad, it's just ... there are all these guys here.
JEFFREY. And we've been through so many of them — memorials. Each one more moving and creative than the last.
STERLING. The Gay Men's Chorus doing Charles Ives.
JEFFREY. Vanessa Redgrave reading Auden.
STERLING. Siegfried and Roy.
JEFFREY. *(Looking across the room.)* Who is that? Talking to Darius?
STERLING. It's Todd Malcolm.
JEFFREY. What?
STERLING. You know, from the gym.
JEFFREY. Oh my God.
STERLING. Jeffrey ...
JEFFREY. He must weigh eighty pounds.

STERLING.　He just got out of the hospital.

JEFFREY.　He's blind, isn't he?

STERLING.　It's a side effect — they think that ninety percent of the vision will return.

JEFFREY.　Oh my God.

STERLING.　Don't stare.

JEFFREY.　Don't stare? When I first came to this city, he was ... a god. I'd never seen anything like that. I used to watch him, dancing with his lover. People would gasp. *(He begins taking off his service jacket.)* I'm sorry.

STERLING.　What are you doing?

JEFFREY.　I can't work here. I can't go to one more of these. I can't see one more twenty-eight-year-old man with a cane.

STERLING.　Don't be ridiculous.

JEFFREY.　What are we doing? Cruising? Giggling? Pretending it's all some sort of hoot? I can't keep passing hors d'oeuvres in a graveyard! I went out with Todd! I just saw him in the hospital, and I don't even recognize him!

STERLING.　Stop it! *(Darius enters, in a dark suit, with a cocktail.)*

DARIUS.　Hi, guys. Did you see Todd?

STERLING.　Of course.

DARIUS.　He looks better.

JEFFREY.　Darius, Todd is dying! *(Darius faces him; Jeffrey realizes his mistake.)* He's ... doing okay, I guess.

DARIUS.　At least he's out of St. Vincent's. I mean, three months! Remember that collage he made on the wall? With all those Armani ads, and anything with Ann-Margret? *(He realizes something is wrong.)* What's going on here?

STERLING.　Jeffrey is just having some sort of anxiety moment.

DARIUS.　About Todd, right? It's okay. Do you know what we were talking about? This memorial. The cannoli are frozen. The drinks are watered. And I hated that singer. At my memorial, I want Liza!

STERLING.　You are not having a memorial.

DARIUS.　I mean, like, in a million years.

STERLING.   You are not going to get sick. I thought I'd made that clear.

DARIUS.   But I *was* sick. I had pneumonia, and it went away. But I want — the Winter Garden. I do! And I want all the other cats to come out ... and sing "Darius" to the tune of "Memory." *(He sings, to the tune of "Memory," while making paw-like gestures.)* "Darius, we all thought you were fabulous ..."

STERLING.   Fine. And the service will run for years.

JEFFREY.   Sterling!

STERLING.   What?

JEFFREY.   I mean ... aren't we all being just a bit much? About all this?

DARIUS.   What do you mean?

JEFFREY.   I mean — it's a memorial.

DARIUS.   So?

JEFFREY.   We're making remarks. We're dishing it.

STERLING.   Really, darling. Picture mine. And Jeffrey, do remember — open coffin. They can say it to my face.

JEFFREY.   *(Viciously.)* Good idea.

DARIUS.   Well, I like it. I mean, cute guys, and Liza, and dish   — it's not a cure for AIDS, Jeffrey. But it's the opposite of AIDS. Right?

STERLING.   Shh, bow your heads. We're supposed to be praying. *(They all bow their heads.)*

JEFFREY.   *(To Sterling.)* What are you praying for?

STERLING.   What do you think? No more disease, no more prejudice.

DARIUS.   And?

STERLING.   *(Glancing around.)* No more chintz.

NURSE'S VOICE.   *(On PA system.)* Scott Elliman to the front desk — Scott Elliman. Visiting hours are over in fifteen minutes. Fifteen minutes. Regular visiting hours are ten A.M. to four thirty. And six to eight P.M. *(Lights fade on the memorial. Lights up on a row of fiberglass waiting-room chairs. There is an exit sign, a sign reading "St. Vincent's," and a metal cart holding an array of medical paraphernalia. Jeffrey sits in one of the chairs. Steve enters; he and Jeffrey see each other.)*

JEFFREY. Are you following me?

STEVE. Of course, I always follow men into clinics.

JEFFREY. How are you?

STEVE. Still positive. Darn.

JEFFREY. Okay …

STEVE. And you? What brings you to St. Vincent's high-profile outpatient facility? White sale?

JEFFREY. Blood test. *(Steve grins and crosses his fingers on both hands.)*

STEVE. I'm sorry. There was one thing I never told you. I'm HIV-positive — and obnoxious.

JEFFREY. I knew.

STEVE. Still no acting work?

JEFFREY. No.

STEVE. Still no day job?

JEFFREY. No.

STEVE. Still no sex?

JEFFREY. Steve.

STEVE. You know, Jeffrey, St. Vincent's is not just another Blue Cross pavilion and biopsy barn. Oh no.

JEFFREY. What is it with you?

STEVE. Oh, I don't know. Being here, in my living room, and seeing you — it's a killer combo. It's just got me all a-tingle. What shall I wear? *(Steve goes to the medical cart and begins holding up various items. His tone is that of a haughty, scintillating host at a fashion show.)* What will today's sassy and sophisticated HIV-positive male be wearing this spring, to tempt the elusive, possibly negative waitperson? Let's begin with the basics — a gown! *(With a flourish, he unfurls a green hospital gown and puts it on over his clothes.)* It's crisp, it's cotton, it's been sterilized over five thousand times — it always works. *(He begins to model the gown, as if on a runway.)* It's a go-nowhere, do-nothing look, with a peekaboo rear and *(Indicating a bloodstain.)* a perky plasma accent. Add pearls and pentamidine, and you're ready for remission!

JEFFREY. Only in green?

STEVE. Please! Green is the navy blue of health care. But it's the accessories that really make the man. Earrings … *(He holds two syringes up to his ears and aims them at Jeffrey.)* Careful! Hat ... *(He places a bed pan on his head as a chapeau; he removes the bed pan and reads the label.)* "Sanicare"! And of course ... *(He holds up two surgical gloves.)* Gloves!

JEFFREY. *(Very entertained, applauding.)* I'll take it!

STEVE. Cash or charge? *(He pretends to take a charge card from Jeffrey.)* Oh no — but according to this, madam is HIV-negative. This is not for you. This is only for a select few, the truly chic, the fashion plates who may not live to see the fall collections.

JEFFREY. Steve ...

STEVE. Can I show you something in — a healthy person? Someone without complications? Someone you could bear to touch?

JEFFREY. Look ...

STEVE. Okay. Okay. Show's over. *(He curtsies.)* Merci.

JEFFREY. Are you all right?

STEVE. *(Tugging off the gown.)* What do you care? Stop being so compassionate. No one's watching.

JEFFREY. Jesus Christ!

STEVE. I'm sorry, I'm a little manic today. And I didn't expect to see you here. I'm being a jerk.

JEFFREY. No, you're fine. I admire your spirit. And your humor.

STEVE. Don't admire me! Fuck me! Admiration gets me an empty dance card, except for the chest X-rays and the occasional march on Washington. Admiration gets me a lovely memorial and a square on the quilt!

NURSE'S VOICE. *(On PA system.)* Jeffrey Calloway to examining room one — Jeffrey Calloway.

STEVE. Your table is ready.

JEFFREY. Do you want to go first?

STEVE. What?

JEFFREY. I don't mind.

STEVE. Jeffrey, I am not here to see the doctor. Surprise!

JEFFREY. You're not?

STEVE. No, I'm on my way to the tenth floor, to see the AIDS babies.

JEFFREY.   Why?

STEVE.   As a volunteer. The last time I was up there, there were eight. They were all abandoned, or their parents had died. And no one would touch them — the nurses were all scared, or busy. The first baby I saw was just lying there, staring, not even crying. But when I held her, she finally smiled and gurgled and acted like a baby. We're all AIDS babies, Jeffrey. And I don't want to die without being held. *(Steve exits. lights fade on the clinic. Jeffrey's dad enters; he is a straightforward midwestern man, in a cardigan and Sansabelt slacks. He is on the phone.)*

DAD.   Well, howdy, stranger. *(To off-stage.)* It's Jeff!

MOM.   *(From off-stage.)* Oh!

JEFFREY.   Can you tell if you're having a nervous breakdown? Or do you just wake up in a strait jacket, and notice the bars on the windows? I called my parents. *(Jeffrey picks up a phone receiver and continues to address the audience.)*

DAD.   Well, isn't this a special occasion!

JEFFREY.   I love them. I mean, I wasn't kicked out or abused or anything. But they still live in Wisconsin, and we just sort of agree not to get too personal.

DAD.   Your mother's right here. *(Jeffrey's mom enters, in a cardigan, a wrap skirt, and sneakers. She is wholesome and sensible.)*

JEFFREY.   But what if I could really talk to them? What if they really had some answers? Or would that just be too weird?

DAD.   So how are things in the Big Apple?

JEFFREY.   *(Into the phone.)* Dad — I've stopped having sex.

DAD.   *(To Mom.)* Eileen, Jeff's stopped having sex.

MOM.   *(Concerned.)* Let me get on the other line. *(She picks up an extension.)* No sex? You mean just safe sex, don't you, dear?

JEFFREY.   No, Mom, I hate safe sex.

DAD.   Wrestling with those condoms.

MOM.   Water-based lubricants.

DAD.   Dry kissing.

MOM.   Sweetheart — are you a top or a bottom?

JEFFREY.   Mother!

DAD.   Have you tried any of those workshops?

MOM.   What about a jerk-off club?

DAD.   How about — phone sex?

JEFFREY.   What?

MOM.   Fred, let's help him out. *(To Jeffrey.)* Darling, what are you wearing?

JEFFREY.   Jeans and a shirt.

DAD.   *(Very matter-of-fact.)* Oh, that's hot.

MOM.   That's very hot.

DAD.   Are you alone?

JEFFREY.   Dad! I am not going to have phone sex with you and Mom!

MOM.   Oh, don't be such a stick-in-the-mud. This is your mother. I've bathed you. I've changed your diapers.

DAD.   Is that what you like?

JEFFREY.   *(Panicking.)* Operator?

MOM.   Darling, you can't just resign from the human race. Have you looked at any videos?

JEFFREY.   Videos?

DAD.   Hard-core. Have you explored masturbation?

MOM.   As if we have to ask. Sometimes I never did get into that bathroom.

DAD.   We like that new Jeff Stryker film. *Powertool II.*

MOM.   Jeff isn't in that one, dear. It's got Lex Baldwin. He's a little short, but he's got beautiful skin. And oh, that scene in the prison laundry!

DAD.   I like Jeff. I say stick with the best. *Powertool. The Young and the Hung.* I'm from Wisconsin.

MOM.   Dear, do you like it when they shave their assholes?

JEFFREY.   Shave their *what?*

DAD.   And what about this fellow Steve? Seems very nice.

JEFFREY.   Dad — Steve is HIV-positive.

MOM.   And a dreamboat. Check the basket. *(Jeffrey hangs up.)*

JEFFREY.   Oh my God. I'm sorry, I'm sorry. That is not really the way it went. *(Mom and Dad switch their phone receivers to opposite ears.)*

DAD.   So, you keeping busy?

JEFFREY.   Oh yes, I worked five nights last week.

MOM.   That big city. It sounds very exciting.

JEFFREY.   Sometimes. So how are you? Doing okay?

DAD.   A touch of arthritis. Can't complain.

MOM.   Have you tried Motrin? We love it!

JEFFREY.   No, not yet.

DAD.   So — when will we see you again?

JEFFREY.   Soon. As soon as I can take some time off. Christmas for sure.

MOM.   I love you.

DAD.   Take care.

JEFFREY.   Dad ... *(Lights down on Mom and Dad. A stained-glass window begins to glow. An altar railing appears. Sacred music is heard. We are in St. Patrick's Cathedral. Jeffrey puts on a jacket and kneels at the railing, his back to the audience. He crosses himself; bows his head, and begins to pray. A priest, Father Dan, enters, wearing the traditional collar and full-length cassock. He kneels beside Jeffrey, crosses himself; bows his head, and begins to pray. After a moment, Father Dan's hand reaches out and grabs Jeffrey's behind. Jeffrey stares at the priest, who withdraws his hand. Both men bow their heads and resume praying. Once again Father Dan's hand reaches out and grabs Jeffrey's behind, with a great deal of conviction. Jeffrey squirms and stares at Father Dan.)* Excuse me? *(Father Dan rises with great dignity. He stands, and motions with his head.)*

FATHER DAN.   Come on. *(Father Dan exits. Jeffrey, quite perplexed, follows him. Lights down on the altar. Lights up on a storeroom somewhere in the cathedral, with piles of hymnals and a Gothic bench. Father Dan enters, followed by Jeffrey. Father Dan is very working-class, a tough, two-fisted guy. He is passionate in his beliefs; he is a dedicated, thoughtful, lusty man, clinging to sanity while surrounded by absurdity and horror. This scene must be played with great ferocity and need; it is not just a chat or debate.)* In here.

JEFFREY.   Where are we?

FATHER DAN.   A storeroom. Some old hymnals. They need to be rebound. *(Father Dan grabs Jeffrey and kisses him. Jeffrey pulls away.)*

JEFFREY.   Hey!

FATHER DAN.   What? What's wrong?

JEFFREY.   *(Stunned.)* Excuse me?

FATHER DAN. Is it the collar? Is that a turn-off? Aren't you Catholic? *(Father Dan makes another lunge at Jeffrey, chasing him around the room. Jeffrey fends him off.)*
JEFFREY. Wait! Are you really a priest?
FATHER DAN. Of course.
JEFFREY. But what's going on? Why did you bring me here?
FATHER DAN. I'm attracted to you. The door's locked.
JEFFREY. Wait — you're a priest? And you cruise guys at St. Patrick's?
FATHER DAN. Yeah! And what were you doing in the pews?
JEFFREY. I was not! Aren't you supposed to be straight? And celibate?
FATHER DAN. Wait — maybe you didn't hear me. I'm a Catholic priest. Historically, that's somewhere in between chorus boy and florist. C'mere. *(Father Dan chases Jeffrey again. Jeffrey pushes him away with great fury.)*
JEFFREY. No! Get away from me! Don't touch me!
FATHER DAN. *(Holding up his hands, backing off.)* All right! All right! I won't! What's wrong? *(Jeffrey tries to pull himself together. During the following speech, his despair, rage, and yearning will overwhelm him.)*
JEFFREY. Two nights ago I was at the ballet, with my friends. It's *Nutcracker*. And it's intermission, and we're walking down this wide marble staircase, and suddenly — Darius falls. He just crumples up, and pitches forward, and keeps tumbling, and his legs are all bent, and there's blood everywhere, and Jesus — he's a dancer! He's just a kid! And he's so dehydrated from some fucking AIDS drug that he can't even stand up! And all the parents are screaming about their kids, and the blood, and we get him into an ambulance, and he's home now, but I've been walking for forty-eight hours! And I finally come here, to church, where I haven't been since I was twelve, and all I keep thinking is — what if it was Steve? How could I love someone, and watch that happen?
FATHER DAN. Wait — who's Darius? Who's Steve?
JEFFREY. *(Exploding.)* Why did He do this? Why did God make the world this way, and why do I have to live in it?

You're a priest — you have to tell me! Don't you?

FATHER DAN.   All right. If I tell you — if I show you the true face of God — will you listen?

JEFFREY.   Of course! That's why I'm here!

FATHER DAN.   Will you really listen?

JEFFREY.   Yes! *(Father Dan sits Jeffrey down.)*

FATHER DAN.   First, here's how you see God. He's a Columbia recording artist.

JEFFREY.   What?

FATHER DAN.   You got your idea of God from where most gay kids get it — the album cover of *My Fair Lady*. Original cast. It's got this Hirschfeld caricature of George Bernard Shaw up in the clouds, manipulating Rex Harrison and Julie Andrews on strings, like marionettes. It was your parents' album, you were little, you thought it was a picture of God. As, I believe, did Shaw. Right?

JEFFREY.   *(Surprised.)* Yeah.

FATHER DAN.   Well, you were almost there. Because God is on that record. Lerner and Loewe! "Why Can't the English." "Wouldn't It Be Loverly." I'm telling you, the only times I really feel the presence of God are when I'm having sex, and during a great Broadway musical!

JEFFREY.   You're nuts.

FATHER DAN.   Excuse me? All you people, you're worshipping resurrections, virgin births, Ben-Hur, and I'm nuts?

JEFFREY.   I'm talking about a plague! About, I don't know — evil!

FATHER DAN.   Yes! Satan! Well, that's another story. I've seen him. He's among us. He's real.

JEFFREY.   What? Disease? Hospitals? Fear?

FATHER DAN.   *Phantom. Miss Saigon. Sunset Boulevard!* Know ye the signs of the devil: overmiking, smoke machines, trouble with Equity.

JEFFREY.   *(Rising to leave.)* Gotta go ...

FATHER DAN.   Why? Because I haven't told you the secret of life, in five words or less? You're getting antsy?

JEFFREY.   I need to know!

FATHER DAN.   Okay, okay. I am so horny! Do you know

what it's like in that confessional? "Father, I abused myself eight times last week." "Father, I'm attracted to my brother-in-law." "Father, I'm having impure thoughts about my soccer coach." Where are the Polaroids? What am I, a mind reader? Say six Hail Marys and bring me his shorts! (*Jeffrey starts to leave again.*) Okay, okay — secret of life. All of those people out there, in the pews, they're not so bad, most of them. They're just like you — you just want a few mindless answers, some autocomfort, and you're a little too uptight for Madame Zora in her storefront. But you've only got one problem — you're completely wrong!

JEFFREY.   I am?

FATHER DAN.   Of course! Who's your God? Some prissy classroom monitor, nodding at the brown-nosers, and smacking anyone who gets out of line? A God who does what — sends us Mussolini and brain cancer to test us, for our own good? That's not God — that's Aunt Betty with an enema!

JEFFREY.   So what — there's no God? It's all just random, luck of the draw, *bad* luck of the draw!

FATHER DAN.   Darling, my darling — have you ever been to a picnic? And someone blows up a balloon, and everyone starts tossing it around? And the balloon drifts and it catches the light, and it's always just about to touch the ground, but someone always gets there just in time, to tap it back up. That balloon — that's God. The very best in all of us. The kindness. The heavy petting. The eleven o'clock numbers.

JEFFREY.   But what about the bad stuff? When the balloon does hit the ground, when it bursts?

FATHER DAN.   Who cares? Evil bores me. It's one-note. It doesn't sing. Of course life sucks; it always will — so why not make the most of it? How dare you not lunge for any shred of happiness?

JEFFREY.   With Steve, who's sick? Who I'm afraid to touch?

FATHER DAN.   So maybe you need a rubber or a surgical mask or a roll of Saran Wrap! But how dare you give up sex, when there are children in Europe who can't get a date! There is only one real blasphemy — the refusal of joy! Of a corsage and a kiss!

JEFFREY. So what're you telling me? Perk up? Look on the sunny side? Get out more?

FATHER DAN. What's your alternative? When did despair become enjoyable? Grief, yes; tears, of course; but terminal gloom? Who does that help? Even Brecht wrote musicals.

JEFFREY. If you believe all this, all this smile-button gospel, if those people out there have it all wrong — then why did you become a priest?

FATHER DAN. I'm working from within. That's why I have to stick around, kiss a few rings, get to be a cardinal. 'Cause the next time we choose a Pope, I've got the guy.

JEFFREY. What? Who?

FATHER DAN. Tommy Tune! Perfect, huh? Someone upbeat? I know it's nuts, of course it's ridiculous — who could afford him? But that's my church — high kicks to heaven.

JEFFREY. *(Backing away.)* You're no priest! I don't know what you are! You're just some sort of lunatic, dressed up in a priest suit!

FATHER DAN. Isn't that redundant? *(Pursuing Jeffrey again.)* Here we go!

JEFFREY. Get away from me!

FATHER DAN. I told you the meaning of life! Now put out! *(Father Julian, an earnest young priest, knocks on the door.)*

FATHER JULIAN. Father Maginnis, please! I don't know what to do! You have to help me!

FATHER DAN. All I wanted was a quickie. *(He opens the door.)* Yes, my son?

FATHER JULIAN. Father, Mass is about to begin. The congregation is starting to worry.

FATHER DAN. Oh, all right! Those people! What would happen if I didn't show up? Animal sacrifice?

FATHER JULIAN. *(Shocked.)* Father!

FATHER DAN. *(To Father Julian.)* You're new. You'll learn. *(To Jeffrey.)* Think about what I said. Will you do that? And call me?

JEFFREY. I can't.

FATHER JULIAN. Father, the altar boys are in place!

FATHER DAN. *(To Father Julian.)* Don't tease. *(Father Dan*

51

and Father Julian exit, followed by Jeffrey. The scenery for the store-
room begins to vanish. Joyous, irresistible disco music is heard. Steve
appears, wearing an official Gay Pride T-shirt. He carries a bullhorn
and a clipboard. We hear parade noise.)

STEVE.   *(Into bullhorn.)* The parade is about to begin! The
first unit will be as follows: Dykes on Bikes! *(The roar of mo-*
torcycles is heard.) Concerned Pan-Asian Bisexuals! *(A cheer is*
heard.) Black Gay Republicans! *(There is no response.)* Hello? *(A*
middle-aged woman runs on. She wears a New Jersey Mafia princess
look: stretch pants, high heels, bouffant hair, outsize sunglasses, lots
of gold jewelry, a quilted lamé bag, and a glitzy sequined sweatshirt
with shoulder pads. Animal prints might also be a favorite. She
speaks with a nasal Jersey accent; she is rowdy and forthright, clearly
a social leader and a take-charge person. She is Mrs. Marcangelo.)

MRS. MARCANGELO.   *(To Steve.)* Excuse me! Are you with
the parade? I'm lost!

STEVE.   No problem. Which group are you with? *(Angelique*
Marcangelo enters. Angelique is the woman's son, in drag, and they
are dressed somewhat alike, overdone and cheery.)

ANGELIQUE.   Ma! Did you find out? *(To Steve.)* We're
marching together.

MRS. MARCANGELO.   *(Sincerely.)* I am so proud of my
preoperative transsexual lesbian son! *(Jeffrey enters, carrying a full*
laundry bag.)

JEFFREY.   Steve.

STEVE.   Jeffrey! We're about to start! Who are you marching with?

MRS. MARCANGELO.   *(To Jeffrey.)* Excuse me — could you
take our picture? With this nice man? *(She hands Jeffrey her cam-*
era and poses with Steve and Angelique.) It's for my album. It's
our first parade!

ANGELIQUE.   We're going to be on a truck!

STEVE.   *(To Jeffrey.)* Parents of Transsexuals.

ANGELIQUE.   Preoperative Transsexual Lesbians.

JEFFREY.   Okay ...

MRS. MARCANGELO.   Believe me —

JEFFREY.   *(Snapping the photo.)* Smile!

MRS. MARCANGELO.   — at first I was as confused as anyone. *(She takes back the camera.)* More confused. When Anthony first came to me —

ANGELIQUE.   Angelique, Ma.

MRS. MARCANGELO.   You were still Tony, at the time. He said, "Ma, I want to be a woman — I've always felt like one." I said, "What, are you gay?" He said, "No, I'm not gay — I'm a lesbian!"

ANGELIQUE.   Exactly!

MRS. MARCANGELO.   And my first thought is, when I was pregnant with you, what did I do? Did I Tilt-a-Whirl? Did I bungee jump?

ANGELIQUE.   But you didn't judge.

MRS. MARCANGELO.   Listen, alone, late at night, I judged plenty. I judged you, I judged me, I said, I don't understand, why does he need this? And you know what made me feel better?

STEVE.   What?

MRS. MARCANGELO.   Those Summer Olympics. I was watching them on TV, feeling sorry for myself. And they kept showing the parents, of all those girls in the pool, those ...

ANGELIQUE.   Synchronized swimmers.

MRS. MARCANGELO.   Exactly. And the parents were all crying, and waving little flags, and I just thought, Hey — if they can be proud of their kids, just because they can stand on their heads in the deep end, then I can be proud of mine! *(Sterling enters, wearing sunglasses and carrying a large, rolled-up banner.)*

STERLING.   Jeffrey! Steven! *(Sterling and Steve kiss.)*

MRS. MARCANGELO.   Look at that — two men kissing! *(She snaps a photo and says to Angelique.)* Why can't you be like that?

ANGELIQUE.   *Ma* ... do we need sunscreen?

MRS. MARCANGELO.   *(Rummaging through her shoulder bag.)* Right here.

STERLING.   Has anyone seen Darius? I lost him somewhere near the S&M people. I swear, I saw this terrifying man, wearing a dog collar, a harness, and jackboots, snarling at me. And I look closer, and it's my upholsterer. *(Darius runs in, wearing a T-shirt, shorts, and boots, very excited.)*

DARIUS.   Should I get my nipples pierced?
STERLING.   What?
DARIUS.   I just saw this big guy, totally naked, except for a jockstrap and two big gold rings, right here and here. *(He gestures on his chest.)*
STERLING.   For guest towels.
MRS. MARCANGELO.   Which group are you with?
STERLING.   Gay Men Who Need a Cigarette. *(Sterling and Darius unfurl their banner, which stretches between them on a pole. The banner is beautifully lettered and decorated with expensive fringe and tassels. Sterling and Darius read aloud the words on the banner.)*
DARIUS.   "Interior Designers Fight AIDS."
STERLING.   "Care with Flair." *(Loud parade noise is heard — bands, motorcycles, disco, etc.)*
STEVE.   We're starting! *(Into bullhorn.)* Parents of Pre-Ops! Prepare to move!
ANGELIQUE.   *(To her mother.)* How do I look?
MRS. MARCANGELO.   *(Tenderly.)* Gorgeous!
ANGELIQUE and MRS. MARCANGELO.   *(Protecting their coiffures as they attempt to hug.)* Hair! *(The Marcangelos exit, very excited.)*
STERLING.   Come along, Jeffrey — help with this thing.
JEFFREY.   *(Holding up his laundry bag.)* Delicate hand washables — I'll catch up.
DARIUS.   All right! *(To Sterling.)* Move it! *(Sterling and Darius exit, carrying their banner.)*
STEVE.   Dump that stuff. I'll put you on the best float — with the porn stars.
JEFFREY.   No, it's okay. I'm not marching.
STEVE.   You're not marching?
JEFFREY.   Not this year. I can't. I am not an asset to this parade.
STEVE.   Jeffrey, I hope this doesn't have anything to do with me. I know I gave you a pretty tough time.
JEFFREY.   You didn't.
STEVE.   I tried. But it really is good to see you. You look great. And I'm not hitting on you.

JEFFREY.   Why not?

STEVE.   Oh, Jeffrey. *(They stare at each other, in an awkward moment of renewed longing.)*

JEFFREY.   I should go. I'm meeting someone.

STEVE.   *(With a leer.)* Pardon me?

JEFFREY. * My sublet. I hope.

STEVE.   Your sublet? Are you moving? Where?

JEFFREY.   It doesn't matter.

STEVE.   *Where?*

JEFFREY.   I shouldn't have said anything!

STEVE.   Come on!

JEFFREY.   Back to Wisconsin.

STEVE.   Wisconsin?

JEFFREY.   Not for a month! I have to go ...

STEVE.   Wait a minute!

JEFFREY.   It's a very good idea! There are no car alarms, no potholes ...

STEVE.   No parades. What about Sterling? And Darius?

JEFFREY.   Don't tell them!

STEVE.   *What?*

JEFFREY.   I'm going to — I just have to find a spare moment, we've all been so busy ...

STEVE.   You are leaving town? Now?

JEFFREY.   Darius is doing much better! He looks great! He's off the Intraconozal, he's gained his weight back ...

STEVE.   You are really a piece of work.

JEFFREY.   *(After a beat.)* Yes I am! I'm a shit, and I'm a coward, and I'm a traitor. And I'm running away, just as fast as my frequent flier miles can carry me! Because if I stay here, I will lose it! And how does that help anyone?

STEVE.   And what are you going to do? In Wisconsin?

JEFFREY.   Live! Breathe! Hide! Until it's all over!

STEVE.   Until what's all over? AIDS? Or your life?

JEFFREY.   *(Very distraught.)* Either.

STEVE.   Good to have known you. A growth experience.

JEFFREY.   Okay, look, maybe I'll come back. Who knows? Someday.

STEVE.   There is the difference between you and me. In

that one word. "Someday." A real luxury item. *(Sean, another marcher, enters. He is attractive and appealing.)*

SEAN.   There you are! *(Sean and Steve kiss. Steve gets rather passionate.)*

STEVE.   Sean, this is Jeffrey.

SEAN.   *(Very friendly.)* Really? At last! I've heard way too much about you!

JEFFREY.   Oh, those tabloids. Are you guys ...?

STEVE.   *(To Sean.)* For what? Two months now?

SEAN.   *(To Jeffrey.)* We met on the parade committee. *(To Steve.)* They need you. *(To Jeffrey.)* Great to meet you. *(Chuck Farling, a TV reporter, enters, in a blazer and a startlingly blond blown-dry hair style. He carries a microphone and speaks to the camera. He is vain and fatuous, very full of himself and his own importance.)*

CHUCK.   *(Adjusting the hidden headset in his ear.)* Yeah, I know we've got to cover this thing, but why me? *(Smiling for the camera.)* Good afternoon, this is Chuck Farling, here at Manhattan's some would say notorious Gay Pride March. Homosexuals have made great strides in recent years, and — I'm surrounded by them. Your names?

STEVE.   Steve Howard.

SEAN.   Sean Bailey.

CHUCK.   And are you ... homosexuals?

STEVE.   Yes, Chuck, we are.

SEAN.   We are righteous members of the Queer Nation!

STEVE.   And you?

CHUCK.   No! Oh no, I'm ... with Channel 9 Action News. *(Sterling and Darius enter and spot Chuck.)*

DARIUS.   *(Crazed.)* Chuck!

CHUCK.   Yes, young man? *(To the camera.)* Another gay marcher.

DARIUS.   I love your show! You are so cute! *(Trying to compose himself, for the camera.)* Hi. We're here, we're queer ... *(Unable to control himself.)* ... and we're on TV!

STERLING.   Chuck, I'm truly sorry. He gets overexcited. *(Sterling has been staring at Chuck's hairpiece. Sterling reaches over and touches Chuck's hair, lightly. Chuck pulls back. Sterling reassures him.)* No, it's working, really.

CHUCK.   Spirits are running very high here in Washington Square! *(He spots Jeffrey.)* And here's a regular fellow — why, he could be anyone, your son, your brother, the guy next door. Your name? *(Chuck strides over to interview Jeffrey. Darius, Sterling, Steve, and Sean all move right along with Chuck; they are all eager to stay on camera. They group themselves behind Sterling and Darius's banner.)*

JEFFREY.   Jeffrey.

CHUCK.   And how are you celebrating Gay Pride Day?

JEFFREY.   I'm … doing my laundry.

STEVE.   His laundry! Just like a regular person! You see, all gays are not flamboyant and overtly … extreme. *(Darius flamboyantly kicks one leg out from behind the banner.)* So you're doing your laundry, here on Gay Pride Day.

JEFFREY.   Yes, Chuck, I am.

CHUCK.   *(To the camera.)* Provocative. *(The Marcangelos enter. They see Chuck and scream. Jeffrey exits.)*

MRS. MARCANGELO.   Chuck!

ANGELIQUE.   Chuck Farling!

MRS. MARCANGELO.   We love you! *(The Marcangelos run over to Chuck and look into the camera.)* Hi, Theresa — hi, Mrs. Russamano — it's us! We're on TV! With Chuck Farling!

CHUCK.   Well, it seems we have a mother-and-daughter team here with us — is that right?

ANGELIQUE.   That's right!

MRS. MARCANGELO.   Don't ask.

CHUCK.   And what are you ladies doing to celebrate this Gay Pride occasion? Something very special?

ANGELIQUE.   You bet, Chuck! We're going to ride on a flatbed truck, for all the world to see!

MRS. MARCANGELO.   Because we are proud of who and what we are!

CHUCK.   And after the parade?

STERLING.   *(Taking Chuck's microphone.)* Angelique is going to remove her penis. *(Everyone cheers, as Chuck looks distinctly uncomfortable and motions with a finger across his throat to his film crew — "Cut!")*

NURSE'S VOICE. *(On PA system.)* Dr. Matthews to ICU — Dr. Matthews. Joel Garber to the front desk — Joel Garber. *(Lights dim on the parade. Lights up on St. Vincent's waiting room. Sterling enters and sits in one of the fiberglass chairs. He is alone. After a beat, Jeffrey enters.)*
JEFFREY.   How is he?
STERLING.   No change.
JEFFREY.   Can I see him?
STERLING.   No. He won't know who you are. Or talk. It's a coma.
JEFFREY.   Do you need anything?
STERLING.   No, I'm okay. Where were you?
JEFFREY.   Working. My last job. The Hilton. A whimper. Is his mom in there?
STERLING.   No. She's back at our place, getting some rest. He doesn't recognize anyone.
JEFFREY.   You never know, for sure —
STERLING.   *(Cutting him off.)* No he doesn't. He's dead.
JEFFREY.   What?
STERLING.   Half an hour ago. I ... that's the first time I've said it. Out loud. A brain hemorrhage. That's why it was so fast. Brain things. That's why three weeks ago, he was marching on Fifth Avenue. With me.
JEFFREY.   Sterling, I am so sorry.
STERLING.   You're what? *(Jeffrey tries to embrace Sterling. Sterling pulls away.)* You're sorry? Thank you, Jeffrey. Thank you. Darius is dead. I'm sorry too. *(He takes a breath, and then, sincerely.)* I'm sorry.
JEFFREY.   Is there anything I can do?
STERLING.   *(Very straightforward, not emotional.)* I wasn't ... enough. I wasn't important enough. I couldn't snub it. I couldn't scare it off, with a look. I couldn't shield him, with raw silk, and tassels, and tiebacks. The limits of style.
JEFFREY.   You loved Darius. He loved you.
STERLING.   Jesus, Jeffrey, how can you?
JEFFREY.   What?
STERLING.   Jeffrey, I don't know why, I'm obviously out of my mind, but right now — no, I don't. I don't hate you.

JEFFREY.   You hate me?
STERLING.   *(Standing, moving away.)* Jeffrey, perhaps you should just not be here. Just right now.
JEFFREY.   Sterling, please — let me help you. What can I do?
STERLING.   What can you do? Nothing! You're leaving. You're going away, to ... someplace insane.
JEFFREY.   I can stay. For a few more days.
STERLING.   No. Please go. You are not part of this. This has nothing to do with you. *(Jeffrey, very upset, starts to leave.)* You know, Darius said he thought you were the saddest person he ever knew.
JEFFREY.   *(Stunned.)* Why did he say that?
STERLING.   Because he was sick. He had a fatal disease. And he was one million times happier than you.
JEFFREY.   *(After a beat.)* You loved Darius. And look what happens. Do you want me to go through this? With Steve?
STERLING.   Yes. *(Mother Teresa appears. She gestures at Sterling; he freezes. She gestures again, and Darius enters, in a dazzling, all white version of his* Cats *costume.)*
DARIUS.   Jeffrey — guess what?
JEFFREY.   Sterling!
DARIUS.   *(Sitting on one of the fiberglass chairs.)* You know that tunnel of light you're supposed to see, right before you die? It really happens! The first person I saw was my Aunt Berniece. She had emphysema. She hugged me and she said *(As Aunt Berniece, crossing his legs, taking a drag on a cigarette and speaking in a gravelly voice)*, "Darling, can you get me a pair for the matinee?"
JEFFREY.   *(Staggered.)* What are you? Some sort of grief-induced hallucination? Are you a symptom? Why did you come back?
DARIUS.   To see you. I figured you got here too late, after I was already in the coma. Did you bring me anything?
JEFFREY.   Um ... flowers!
DARIUS.   *(Looking around.)* Where?
JEFFREY.   I was in a hurry!
DARIUS.   Jeffrey, I'm dead. You're not.

JEFFREY.   I know that.

DARIUS.   You do? Prove it.

JEFFREY.   What do you mean?

DARIUS.   Go dancing. Go to a show. Make trouble. Make out. Hate AIDS, Jeffrey. Not life.

JEFFREY.   How?

DARIUS.   Just think of AIDS as ... the guest that won't leave. The one we all hate. But you have to remember.

JEFFREY.   What?

DARIUS.   Hey — it's still our party. *(We hear an orchestra tuning up. Darius stands.)* That's the orchestra. I have to go.

JEFFREY.   But ... but is that it? Is that all you can tell me?

DARIUS.   Be nice to Sterling. *(Mother Teresa gestures. Gorgeous romantic music begins, perhaps the Gershwins' "Embraceable You."* Sterling unfreezes. He and Darius gaze at each other and smile. The music swells.)* See you! I'm on. *(Darius exits. Sterling exits in the opposite direction. The lights change. The skyline of Manhattan appears, beneath a glorious full moon. A railing and perhaps a telescopic viewer appear. The clinic vanishes; we are now on the observation deck of the Empire State Building. There is a sports jacket hanging over the railing. A red balloon is also attached to the railing. Mother Teresa helps Jeffrey into the jacket; she checks his appearance. She hands him the balloon. She exits. Steve enters, looking around.)*

STEVE.   Jeffrey?

JEFFREY.   Steve! You showed up!

STEVE.   What is this? A scavenger hunt? Am I on a list? "Meet Steve on the top of the Empire State Building"?

JEFFREY.   I wasn't sure you'd come, when I left the message. I didn't know if ... John would let you.

STEVE.   Sean. Have you seen Sterling?

JEFFREY.   Yeah. He's doing okay. He liked the memorial.

STEVE.   So did I.

STEVE and JEFFREY.   *(After a beat, they sing softly to the tune*

---

* See Special Note on Songs and Recordings on copyright page.

of "Memory.") "DARIUS, WE ALL THOUGHT YOU WERE
FABULOUS ..."
STEVE.   Nice balloon.
JEFFREY.   It was a gift.
STEVE.   And what are you still doing here? I thought you
were headed west, or north.
JEFFREY.   I need a favor.
STEVE.   This is very Hitchcock.
JEFFREY.   I have to ask you something.
STEVE.   And your phone was shut off. Gay castration.
JEFFREY.   Be serious. Can I ask you my favor?
STEVE.   I'm here.
JEFFREY.   Dump Sean.
STEVE.   What?
JEFFREY.   Leave him. Tell him it's over. Be really mean.
STEVE.   It's a little late for that!
JEFFREY.   Why?
STEVE.   He's gone. He ... dumped me.
JEFFREY.   He did? *Really?*
STEVE.   Oh, calm down. He couldn't take it. The sex. He
was exhausted. He's twenty-two.
JEFFREY.   Were you upset?
STEVE.   Of course!
JEFFREY.   A whole bunch?
STEVE.   Jeffrey!
JEFFREY.   Steve, if I asked you to, could we have sex? Safe
sex? Some kind of sex? Tonight?
STEVE   On the top of the Empire State Building?
JEFFREY.   Wherever. I needed ... a moon. You haven't an-
swered my question.
STEVE.   Wait a minute! What is this? You think it's so easy?
You leave a message, snap your fingers? Jeffrey, I'm still HIV-
positive.
JEFFREY.   So?
STEVE.   So — it doesn't go away! It only gets worse!
JEFFREY.   I know.
STEVE.   Don't do this. Don't pretend. I will not be your
good deed!

61

JEFFREY.   Oh, you're not. I'm too selfish. I don't want a red ribbon. I want you.

STEVE.   Say we have sex. Say we like it. And say tomorrow morning you decide to take off, for Wisconsin!

JEFFREY.   I won't!

STEVE.   How do I know that?

JEFFREY.   Because I'm a gay man. And I live in the city. And I'm not an innocent bystander. Not anymore. *(Steve is now somewhat convinced. He studies Jeffrey for a moment.)*

STEVE.   So ... how bad do you want it?

JEFFREY.   Find out.

STEVE.   I like this. This is nice. You want it. Suddenly it's my decision. I get to be Jeffrey.

JEFFREY.   Fuck you.

STEVE.   Maybe.

JEFFREY.   *Maybe?*

STEVE.   You know, I think you should woo me. Maybe dinner. Maybe dancing.

JEFFREY.   Yes!

STEVE.   And then ...

JEFFREY.   Unbelievably hot sex!

STEVE.   Not yet.

JEFFREY.   *(Very frustrated.)* What do you want?

STEVE.   Jewelry.

JEFFREY.   Yes!

STEVE.   No, wait. What did my horoscope say this morning? "You will meet an incredibly fucked-up guy. Happiness is impossible. Go for it."

JEFFREY.   Yes! *(After a beat.)* Yes?

STEVE.   *(After a moment.)* Yes.

JEFFREY.   But Steve — first you have to promise me something.

STEVE.   *(Exasperated.)* *What?*

JEFFREY.   Promise me ... you won't get sick.

STEVE.   *(After a beat.)* Done.

JEFFREY.   And you won't die.

STEVE.   Never.

JEFFREY.   *(Staring at Steve, very emotional.)* Liar. *(Jeffrey and*

Steve move toward each other. Steve pulls back.)
STEVE.　　Jesus. We shouldn't do this. We are really asking for it. Give me one good reason. Give me one reason why we even have a prayer.
JEFFREY.　　You want one good reason?
STEVE.　　I do.
JEFFREY.　　*(After a beat.)* I dare you. *(They stare at each other. Jeffrey tosses the balloon to Steve. The balloon almost hits the ground, but Steve leans forward and catches it. He holds the balloon for a moment and then tosses it back to Jeffrey. They move U. and toward each other, tapping the balloon back and forth. The balloon is caught in the light of the moon and glows translucently. Finally, Jeffrey catches the balloon. He and Steve embrace and kiss as the lights dim.)*

CURTAIN

PROPERTY LIST

Slides of:
    Manhattan skyline
    Greenwich Village
    brownstone
    erotic males
    big garish prizes
    "IT'S JUST SEX"
    "SEXUAL COMPULSIVES ANONYMOUS"
3 Walkmans (GYM RATS #1, #2, and #3)
4 barbells on supports (JEFFREY, GYM RATS #1, #2 and #3, STEVE)
2 forty-five pound barbell weights (STEVE, JEFFREY)
2 expensive sweaters (SALESMAN)
Jacket (SALESMAN, JEFFREY, MOTHER TERESA)
Shopping bag (SALESMAN)
Game show questions on cards (SHOWGIRL)
Dozen roses (SHOWGIRL)
Rhinestone tiara (SHOWGIRL)
Clipboard (CASTING DIRECTOR, STEVE)
Script pages (CASTING DIRECTOR)
Beaded headband with feather (WAITER, JEFFREY, STEVE)
Waiter's tray (JEFFREY, WAITER)
Glass-shaped cowboy boot glass (STEVE)
Bar accessories (STEVE) including:
    vodka bottle
    wine bottle
    club soda
    ice bucket filled with cubes
    lemon/lime slices
    tomato juice
    glassware
Bottle of champagne (STEVE)
2 champagne glasses (STEVE)
Hobbyhorse (ANN)
Cowboy pistols (ANN)

Cigarette (STERLING)
2 cocktails (STERLING, DARIUS)
Bouquet of flowers (STEVE)
Hand-held microphone (DEBRA)
Crocheted baby booties (ACOLYTE #2)
2 whistles on thongs (STERLING, DARIUS)
2 walkie-talkies (STERLING, DARIUS)
Microphone (DEBRA, CHUCK, JEFFREY)
Medical cart (STEVE) with medical paraphernalia:
 green hospital gown with blood stains
 2 syringes
 bedpan
 surgical gloves
Bullhorn (STEVE)
Full laundry bag (JEFFREY)
Camera (MRS. MARCANGELO)
Large, rolled up banner (STERLING, DARIUS)
Large shoulder bag (MRS. MARCANGELO) with:
 sunscreen
Red balloon (MOTHER TERESA, JEFFREY)

COSTUME LIST

ACT ONE

JEFFREY

TOP OF SHOW	White thong White underwear (Calvin Klein) White socks
GYM	Black shorts Grey T-shirt Hi top sneakers
BARNEYS	White dress shirt Jeans with belt Black Rockport loafers
GAMESHOW	Same as Barneys
Audition	Same as above
HOE-DOWN	Add waiter jacket and headband (Scott gives him onstage)
APARTMENT	Lose jacket and headband (onstage at end of dance)
DEBRA MOORHOUSE	Same as above
BEATS ALL	Remove white dress shirt
PINK PANTHERS	Same as above
STREET	Same

| THUGS | Same |
| MOTHER TERESA | Same |

MAN #1, etc.

TOP OF SHOW	Jock strap Grey underwear
GYM	Blue tank top Yellow sorts Tube socks High-top sneakers Black lifting belt

GAMESHOW	Skip wig (with topstick)
	Rigged dickie
	    (under dress green turtleneck,
	    black jeans, black socks, black
	    loafers)
	Pink tuxedo ensemble

CASTING DIRECTOR	Lose wig and tuxedo Green turtleneck Black jeans Black socks Loafers Add: flight jacket Add: baseball cap
HOE-DOWN	White shirt Waiter jacket Breastplate Headdress

DEBRA MOORHOUSE	Chinos
	Multicolored sweater
	Suede loafers
	(underdress: leather jock and
	harness)
BEATS ALL	Leather jock
	Harness
	Chaps
	Boots
	Moustache
THUGS	"U2" T-shirt
	Black jeans
	Cranberry sweatshirt
	Black jacket
	Black cap
	High-top sneakers (same as gym)

MAN #2, etc.

TOP OF SHOW	White biker shorts
	White tank top
	Jock
GYM	White socks
	Black socks (underdressed)
	Blue and yellow striped body suit
	Red high-top sneakers
BARNEYS	Lose shoes
	White socks
	White dress shirt
	Pinstripe jacket
	Pants with belt
	Lavender tie
	Loafers

GAMESHOW	Same as Barneys
HOE-DOWN	Waiter jacket Pants (poly) Brown cowboy hat
DEBRA MOORHOUSE	Black T-shirt Black vest Same suit pants Black glasses Loafers
BEATS ALL	Jock strap (same) Leather jacket Cap Combat boots
THUGS	Bullet hole smiley T-shirt Multicolored patch jeans Red sweatshirt Hooded jacket Boots

STEVE

TOP OF SHOW	Gloves Surgical mask Socks White G string High-top canvas tennis shoes Saran Wrap
GYM	Red T-Shirt Black shorts (Calvin Klein long briefs) Brown lifting belt Same shoes and socks as top of show

HOE-DOWN	Black jeans
	Black belt
	Waiter jacket
	White dress shirt
	Red cowboy hat
	Blue bandana
APARTMENT	Stone-washed red Oxford shirt
	Black jeans
	Black leather jacket
	White socks
	High-top sneakers
STREET	Red T-shirt
	Black jeans

MAN #3, etc.

TOP OF SHOW	Dalmation pajamas
	Jockstrap (under-dress)
	(Chelsea gym tank under
	dress)
GYM	Blue sweatpants
	Chelsea gym tank (under-dress)
	Tube socks
	Tennis shoes
	Yellow nylon lifting belt
BEATS ALL	Black leather pants
	Black vest
	Black cap
	Brown boots
	Moustache

STERLING

TOP OF SHOW	Black shorts "Fuck" bandana Torn white T-shirt
BARNEYS	Beige shirt Linen slacks with belt Beige loafers
APARTMENT	Gaultier shirt Polka dot pants Black loafers
PINK PANTHERS	Beret Pink Panther T-shirt Whistle on pink string Fanny pack with walkie-talkie Grey rayon pants with belt Black socks Black loafers

DARIUS

TOP OF SHOW	Grey bikini briefs White baseball cap
APARTMENT	Brown cat suit with tail and collar Dance belt Overcoat Black slip-ons
PINK PANTHERS	White jeans Black belt Doc Marten boots Tube socks

Pink Panther T-shirt
Beret
Whistle on pink string

ANN MARWOOD BARTLE

TOP OF SHOW

Slut wig
White slip
Black hose
White ballet slippers
Strapless bra

MOTHER TERESA

Cassock
Sari
Hood
Shower cap
No wig

GAMESHOW

Blonde wig
Blue-pleated dress
Black slip-ons

HOE-DOWN

Black beaded and plaid dress
(with 2 ribbons and
diamond pin)
Wig
Earrings and necklace
Holster with 2 guns
Gloves

DEBRA MOORHOUSE

Green/white rayon top and pants
Black shell
Bronze shoes

MOTHER TERESA

Same as previous Mother Teresa

ACT TWO

JEFFREY

SEXUAL COMPULSIVES	White dress suit Underdress grey T-shirt Black bow tie Black jeans with belt White socks Black loafers
MEMORIAL	Add waiter jacket (Remove on stage during scene)
1ST ST. VINCENT'S	Remove tie (on stage)
MOM AND DAD	Same
ST. PATRICK'S (BOTH)	Add tweed jacket
PARADE	Lose white shirt and jacket
2ND ST. VINCENT'S	Add white shirt back on
EMPIRE	Add blue jacket from stage

DARIUS

MEMORIAL	Suit White shirt Tie Black socks Loafers

PARADE	Madonna T-shirt with pins
	Rainbow necklace
	Jeans shorts with belt
	White socks
	Boots

2ND ST. VINCENT'S	White cat suit
	Arms
	Legs
	Collar
	Tail
	White ballet slippers

MAN #1, etc.

SEXUAL COMPULSIVES	Red slime shirt
	Old jeans
	Old jacket
	White socks
	Tennis shoes

PARADE	Cat print pants
	Jewelry
	Purse
	Bomber jacket
	Wig
	Glasses

STEVE

1ST ST. VINCENT'S	Red romantic shirt
	Black jeans with belt
	Tube socks
	Converse

PARADE	Red plaid cutoff shirt
EMPIRE	Black T-shirt
	Red letter jacket

MAN #2, etc.

ST. PATRICK'S	Cloak
	Collar
PARADE	Under dress (orange/gray strip shirt)
	Long jeans shorts
	Black belt
	Black cap with stripes
	Black boots
	White socks

MAN #3, etc.

SEXUAL COMPULSIVES	Chartreuse suit with belt
	Black Gap T-shirt
	Dark socks
	Loafers
MOM AND DAD	Blue Izod shirt
	Grey pants with belt
	Blue sweater
	Wig
	Glasses
ST. PATRICK'S	Cloak
	Collar
	(Very quick change)

PARADE	Blonde wig
	Red jacket
	Red stripe tie
	White shirt

STERLING

MEMORIAL	Pin-striped suit
	Black shirt
	Dark socks
	Loafers
PARADE	Beige Polo shirt
	Sunglasses
	Linen pants
	Brown loafers
2ND ST. VINCENT'S	Add green jacket

ANN MARWOOD BARTLE

SEXUAL COMPULSIVES	Plaid shirt
	Jeans
	Birkenstock shoes
	Socks
MOM AND DAD	Blue knit shirt
	Blue sweater
	Jean skirt
	Pink sneakers
PARADE	Gold lycra leggings
	Leopard print lycra top
	Gold shoes
	Purse
	Jewelry
	Sunglasses
	Wig

SOUND EFFECTS

Music on Walkman:
    hip-hop, throbbing disco, opera
Raucous music
Canned applause
Gameshow buzzer noise
Wild, crazy gameshow "winning" music
Frenzied applause
Country-western dance tune
Doorbell
Phone ringing
Steve's answering machine message
Jeffrey's voice on Steve's answering machine
Heavy iron door slamming
Locks turning
Shrill whistle blast
Beeper on walkie-talkie
Siren (distant, then louder)
Nurse's voice on hospital PA system
Sacred church music
Loud parade music
Roar of motorcycles
Cheer from crowd
Knock on door
Joyous disco music
Orchestra tuning up
Romantic music

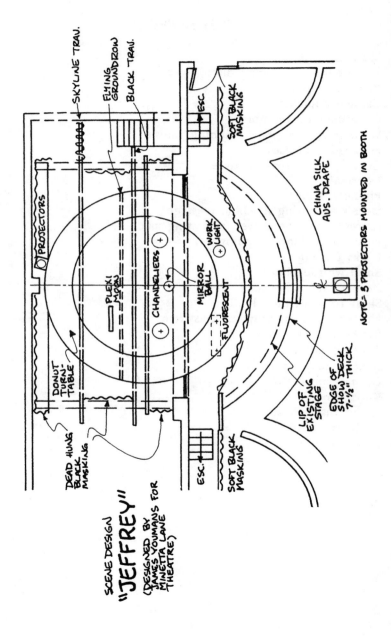

SCENE DESIGN
"JEFFREY"

(DESIGNED BY
JAMES YOUMANS FOR
MINETTA LANE
THEATRE)

SKYLINE TRAV.

FLYING GROUNDROW

BLACK TRAV.

ESC.

SOFT BLACK MASKING

PROJECTORS

PLEXI MOON

CHANDELIERS

MIRROR BALL

WORK LIGHT

FLUORESCENT

CHINA SILK
AUS. DRAPE

NOTE:- 5 PROJECTORS MOUNTED IN BOOTH

DONUT TURN-TABLE

DEAD HUNG
BLACK
MASKING

ESC.

SOFT BLACK
MASKING

LIP OF
EXISTING
STAGE

EDGE OF
SHOW DECK
7-½" THICK